# HISTORY OF JULIUS CAESAR
## BY
Jacob Abbott

# HISTORY OF JULIUS CAESAR

Published by Dossier Press

New York City, NY

First published circa 1879

Copyright © Dossier Press, 2015

All rights reserved

# ABOUT DOSSIER PRESS

Since the moment people have been writing, they've been writing non-fiction works, from the *Histories* of Herodotus to the Code of Hammurabi. **Dossier Press** publishes all of the classic non-fiction works ever written and makes them available to new and old readers alike at the touch of a button.

## PREFACE.

It is the object of this series of histories to present a clear, distinct, and connected narrative of the lives of those great personages who have in various ages of the world made themselves celebrated as leaders among mankind, and, by the part they have taken in the public affairs of great nations, have exerted the widest influence on the history of the human race. The end which the author has had in view is twofold: first, to communicate such information in respect to the subjects of his narratives as is important for the general reader to possess; and, secondly, to draw such moral lessons from the events described and the characters delineated as they may legitimately teach to the people of the present age. Though written in a direct and simple style, they are intended for, and addressed to, minds possessed of some considerable degree of maturity, for such minds only can fully appreciate the character and action which exhibits itself, as nearly all that is described in these volumes does, in close combination with the conduct and policy of governments, and the great events of international history.

# JULIUS CAESAR.: CHAPTER I.: MARIUS AND SYLLA.

Three great European nations of antiquity.

There were three great European nations in ancient days, each of which furnished history with a hero: the Greeks, the Carthaginians, and the Romans.

Alexander.

Alexander was the hero of the Greeks. He was King of Macedon, a country lying north of Greece proper. He headed an army of his countrymen, and made an excursion for conquest and glory into Asia. He made himself master of all that quarter of the globe, and reigned over it in Babylon, till he brought himself to an early grave by the excesses into which his boundless prosperity allured him. His fame rests on his triumphant success in building up for himself so vast an empire, and the admiration which his career has always excited among mankind is heightened by the consideration of his youth, and of the noble and generous impulses which strongly marked his character.

Hannibal.

His terrible energy.

The Carthaginian hero was Hannibal. We class the Carthaginians among the European nations of antiquity; for, in respect to their origin, their civilization, and all their commercial and political relations, they belonged to the European race, though it is true that their capital was on the African side of the Mediterranean Sea. Hannibal was the great Carthaginian hero. He earned his fame by the energy and implacableness of his hate. The work of his life was to keep a vast empire in a state of continual anxiety and terror for fifty years, so that his claim to greatness and glory rests on the determination, the perseverance, and the success with which he fulfilled his function of being, while he lived, the terror of the world.

Julius Caesar.

The Roman hero was Caesar. He was born just one hundred years before the Christian era. His renown does not depend, like that of Alexander, on foreign conquests, nor, like that of Hannibal, on the terrible energy of his aggressions upon foreign foes, but upon his protracted and dreadful contests with, and ultimate triumphs over, his rivals and competitors at home. When he appeared upon the stage, the Roman empire already included nearly all of the world that was worth possessing. There were no more conquests to be made. Caesar did, indeed, enlarge, in some degree, the boundaries of the empire; but the main question in his day was, who should possess the power which preceding conquerors had acquired.

The ancient Roman empire.

The provinces.

The Roman empire, as it existed in those days, must not be conceived of by the reader as united together under one compact and consolidated government. It was, on the other hand, a vast congeries of nations, widely dissimilar in every respect from each other, speaking various languages, and having various customs and laws. They were all, however, more or less dependent upon, and connected with, the great central power. Some of these countries were provinces, and were governed by officers appointed and sent out by the authorities at Rome. These governors had to collect the taxes of their provinces, and also to preside over and direct, in many important respects, the administration of justice. They had, accordingly, abundant opportunities to enrich themselves while thus in office, by collecting more money than they paid over to the government at home, and by taking bribes to favor the rich man's cause in court. Thus the more wealthy and prosperous provinces were objects of great competition among aspirants for office at Rome. Leading men would get these appointments, and, after remaining long enough in their provinces to acquire a fortune, would come back to Rome, and expend it in intrigues and maneuvers to obtain higher offices still.

Foreign wars.

The victorious general.

Whenever there was any foreign war to be carried on with a distant nation or tribe, there was always a great eagerness among all the military officers of the state to be appointed to the command. They each felt sure that they should conquer in the contest, and they could enrich themselves still more rapidly by the spoils of victory in war, than by extortion and bribes in the government of a province in peace. Then, besides, a victorious general coming back to Rome always found that his military renown added vastly to his influence and power in the city. He was welcomed with celebrations and triumphs; the people flocked to see him and to shout his praise. He placed his trophies of victory in the temples, and entertained the populace with games and shows, and with combats of gladiators or of wild beasts, which he had brought home with him for this purpose in the train of his army. While he was thus enjoying his triumph, his political enemies would be thrown into the back ground and into the shade; unless, indeed, some one of them might himself be earning the same honors in some other field, to come back in due time, and claim his share of power and celebrity in his turn. In this case, Rome would be sometimes distracted and rent by the conflicts and contentions of military rivals, who had acquired powers too vast for all the civil influences of the Republic to regulate or control.

ROMAN PLEBEIANS.

Military rivals.

Marius and Sylla.

The patricians and plebeians.

Civil contests.

Quarrel about the command of the army.

Sylla's violence.

There had been two such rivals just before the time of Caesar, who had filled the world with their quarrels. They were Marius and Sylla. Their very names have been, in all ages of the world, since their day, the symbols of rivalry and hate. They were the representatives respectively of the two great parties into which the Roman state, like every other community in which the population at large have any voice in governing, always has been, and probably always will be divided, the upper and the lower; or, as they were called in those days, the patrician and the plebeian. Sylla was the patrician; the higher and more aristocratic portions of the community were on his side. Marius was the favorite of the plebeian masses. In the contests, however, which they waged with each other, they did not trust to the mere influence of votes. They relied much more upon the soldiers they could gather under their respective standards and upon their power of intimidating, by means of them, the Roman assemblies. There was a war to be waged with Mithridates, a very powerful Asiatic monarch, which promised great opportunities for acquiring fame and plunder. Sylla was appointed to the command. While he was absent, however, upon some campaign in Italy, Marius contrived to have the decision reversed, and the command transferred to him Two officers, called tribunes, were sent to Sylla's camp to inform him of the change. Sylla killed the officers for daring to bring him such a message, and began immediately to march toward Rome. In retaliation for the murder of the tribunes, the party of Marius in the city killed some of Sylla's prominent friends there, and a general alarm spread itself throughout the population. The Senate, which was a sort of House of Lords, embodying mainly the power and influence of the patrician party, and was, of course, on Sylla's side, sent out to him, when he had arrived within a few miles of the city, urging him to come no further. He pretended to comply; he marked out the ground for a camp; but he did not, on that account, materially delay his march. The next morning he was in possession of the city. The friends of Marius attempted to resist him, by throwing stones upon his troops from the roofs of the houses. Sylla ordered every house from which these symptoms of resistance appeared to be set on fire. Thus the whole population of a vast and wealthy city were thrown into a condition of extreme danger and terror, by the conflicts of two great bands of armed men, each claiming to be their friends.

Defeat of Marius.

Marius was conquered in this struggle, and fled for his life. Many of the friends whom he left behind him were killed. The Senate were assembled, and, at Sylla's orders, a decree was passed declaring Marius a public enemy, and offering a reward to any one who would bring his head back to Rome.

His flight.

Marius fled, friendless and alone, to the southward, hunted every where by men who were eager to get the reward offered for his head. After various romantic adventures and narrow escapes, he succeeded in making his way across the Mediterranean Sea, and found at last a refuge in a hut among the ruins of Carthage. He was an old man, being now over seventy years of age.

Return of Marius.

He marches against Rome.

Of course, Sylla thought that his great rival and enemy was now finally disposed of, and he accordingly began to make preparations for his Asiatic campaign. He raised his army, built and equipped a fleet, and went away. As soon as he was gone, Marius's friends in the city began to come forth, and to take measures for reinstating themselves in power. Marius returned, too, from Africa, and soon gathered about him a large army. Being the friend, as he pretended, of the lower classes of society, he collected vast multitudes of revolted slaves, outlaws, and other desperadoes, and advanced toward Rome. He assumed, himself, the dress, and air, and savage demeanor of his followers. His countenance had been rendered haggard and cadaverous partly by the influence of exposures, hardships, and suffering upon his advanced age, and partly by the stern and moody plans and determinations of revenge which his mind was perpetually revolving. He listened to the deputations which the Roman Senate sent out to him from time to time, as he advanced toward the city, but refused to make any terms. He moved forward with all the outward deliberation and calmness suitable to his years, while all the ferocity of a tiger was burning within.

Executions by order of Marius.

As soon as he had gained possession of the city, he began his work of destruction. He first beheaded one of the consuls, and ordered his head to be set up, as a public spectacle, in the most conspicuous place in the city. This was the beginning. All the prominent friends of Sylla, men of the highest rank and station, were then killed, wherever they could be found, without sentence, without trial, without any other accusation, even, than the military decision of Marius that they were his enemies, and must die. For those against whom he felt any special animosity, he contrived some special mode of execution. One, whose fate he wished particularly to signalize, was thrown down from the Tarpeian Rock.

The Tarpeian Rock.

The Tarpeian Rock was a precipice about fifty feet high, which is still to be seen in Rome, from which the worst of state criminals were sometimes thrown. They were taken up to the top by a stair, and were then hurled from the summit, to die miserably, writhing in agony after their fall, upon the rocks below.

The story of Tarpeia.

Subterranean passages.

The Tarpeian Rock received its name from the ancient story of Tarpeia. The tale is, that Tarpeia was a Roman girl, who lived at a time in the earliest periods of the Roman history, when the city was besieged by an army from are of the neighboring nations. Besides their shields, the story is that the soldiers had golden bracelets upon their arms. They wished Tarpeia to open the gates and let them in. She promised to do so if they would give her their bracelets; but, as she did not know the name of the shining ornaments, the language she used to designate them was, "Those things you have upon your arms." The soldiers acceded to her terms; she opened the gates, and they, instead of giving her the bracelets, threw their shields upon her as they passed, until the poor girl was crushed down with them and destroyed. This was near the Tarpeian Rock, which afterward took her name. The rock is now found to be perforated by a great many subterranean passages, the remains, probably, of ancient quarries. Some of these galleries are now walled up; others are open; and the people who live around the spot believe, it is said, to this day, that Tarpeia herself sits, enchanted, far in the interior of these caverns, covered with gold and jewels, but that whoever attempts to find her is fated by an irresistible destiny to lose his way, and he never returns. The last story is probably as true as the other.

Escape of Sylla's wife.

Marius continued his executions and massacres until the whole of Sylla's party had been slain or put to flight. He made every effort to discover Sylla's wife and child, with a view to destroying them also, but they could not be found. Some friends of Sylla, taking compassion on their innocence and helplessness, concealed them, and thus saved Marius from the commission of one intended crime. Marius was disappointed, too, in some other cases, where men whom he had intended to kill destroyed themselves to baffle his vengeance. One shut himself up in a room with burning charcoal, and was suffocated with the fumes. Another bled himself to death upon a public altar, calling down the judgments of the god to whom he offered this dreadful sacrifice, upon the head of the tyrant whose atrocious cruelty he was thus attempting to evade.

Illness of Marius.

Sylla outlawed.

By the time that Marius had got fairly established in his new position, and was completely master of Rome, and the city had begun to recover a little from the shock and consternation produced by his executions, he fell sick. He was attacked with an acute disease of great violence. The attack was perhaps produced, and was certainly aggravated by, the great mental excitements through which he had passed during his exile, and in the entire change of fortune which had attended his return. From being a wretched fugitive, hiding for his life among gloomy and desolate ruins, he found himself suddenly transferred to the mastery of the world. His mind was excited, too, in respect to Sylla, whom he had not yet reached or subdued, but who was still prosecuting his war against Mithridates. Marius had had him pronounced by the Senate an enemy to his country, and was meditating plans to reach him in his distant province, considering his triumph incomplete as long as his great rival was at liberty and alive. The sickness cut short these plans, but it only inflamed to double violence the excitement and the agitations which attended them.

Marius delirious.

Death of Marius.

As the dying tyrant tossed restlessly upon his bed, it was plain that the delirious ravings which he began soon to utter were excited by the same sentiments of insatiable ambition and ferocious hate whose calmer dictates he had obeyed when well. He imagined that he had succeeded in supplanting Sylla in his command, and that he was himself in Asia at the head of his armies. Impressed with this idea, he stared wildly around; he called aloud the name of Mithridates; he shouted orders to imaginary troops; he struggled to break away from the restraints which the attendants about his bedside imposed, to attack the phantom foes which haunted him in his dreams. This continued for several days, and when at last nature was exhausted by the violence of these paroxysms of phrensy, the vital powers which had been for seventy long years spending their strength in deeds of selfishness, cruelty, and hatred, found their work done, and sunk to revive no more.

Return of Sylla.

Marius's son.

Proscriptions and massacres of Sylla.

Marius left a son, of the same name with himself, who attempted to retain his father's power;

but Sylla, having brought his war with Mithridates to a conclusion, was now on his return from Asia, and it was very evident that a terrible conflict was about to ensue. Sylla advanced triumphantly through the country, while Marius the younger and his partisans concentrated their forces about the city, and prepared for defense. The people of the city were divided, the aristocratic faction adhering to the cause of Sylla, while the democratic influences sided with Marius. Political parties rise and fall, in almost all ages of the world, in alternate fluctuations, like those of the tides. The faction of Marius had been for some time in the ascendency, and it was now its turn to fall. Sylla found, therefore, as he advanced, every thing favorable to the restoration of his own party to power. He destroyed the armies which came out to oppose him. He shut up the young Marius in a city not far from Rome, where he had endeavored to find shelter and protection, and then advanced himself and took possession of the city. There he caused to be enacted again the horrid scenes of massacre and murder which Marius had perpetrated before, going, however, as much beyond the example which he followed as men usually do in the commission of crime. He gave out lists of the names of men whom he wished to have destroyed, and these unhappy victims of his revenge were to be hunted out by bands of reckless soldiers, in their dwellings, or in the places of public resort in the city, and dispatched by the sword wherever they could be found. The scenes which these deeds created in a vast and populous city can scarcely be conceived of by those who have never witnessed the horrors produced by the massacres of civil war. Sylla himself went through with this work in the most cool and unconcerned manner, as if he were performing the most ordinary duties of an officer of state. He called the Senate together one day, and, while he was addressing them, the attention of the Assembly was suddenly distracted by the noise of outcries and screams in the neighboring streets from those who were suffering military execution there. The senators started with horror at the sound. Sylla, with an air of great composure and unconcern, directed the members to listen to him, and to pay no attention to what was passing elsewhere. The sounds that they heard were, he said, only some correction which was bestowed by his orders on certain disturbers of the public peace.

Executions.

Extent of Sylla's proscriptions.

Man's nature.

Sylla's orders for the execution of those who had taken an active part against him were not confined to Rome. They went to the neighboring cities and to distant provinces, carrying terror and distress every where. Still, dreadful as these evils were, it is possible for us, in the conceptions which we form, to overrate the extent of them. In reading the history of the Roman empire during the civil wars of Marius and Sylla, one might easily imagine that the whole population of the country was organized into the two contending armies, and were employed wholly in the work of fighting with and massacring each other. But nothing like this can be true. It is obviously but a small part, after all, of an extended community that can be ever actively and personally engaged in these deeds of violence and blood. Man is not naturally a ferocious wild beast. On the contrary, he loves, ordinarily, to live in peace and quietness, to till his lands and tend his flocks, and to enjoy the blessings of peace and repose. It is comparatively but a small number in any age of the world, and in any nation, whose passions of ambition, hatred, or revenge become so strong as that they love bloodshed and war. But these few, when they once get weapons into their hands, trample recklessly and mercilessly upon the rest. One ferocious human tiger, with a spear or a bayonet to brandish, will tyrannize as he pleases over a hundred quiet men, who are armed only with shepherds' crooks, and whose only desire is to live in peace with their wives and their children.

Husbandmen.

How the Roman edifices were built.

Standing armies.

Thus, while Marius and Sylla, with some hundred thousand armed and reckless followers, were carrying terror and dismay wherever they went, there were many millions of herdsmen and husbandmen in the Roman world who were dwelling in all the peace and quietness they could command, improving with their peaceful industry every acre where corn would ripen or grass grow. It was by taxing and plundering the proceeds of this industry that the generals and soldiers, the consuls and praetors, and proconsuls and propraetors, filled their treasuries, and fed their troops, and paid the artisans for fabricating their arms. With these avails they built the magnificent edifices of Rome, and adorned its environs with sumptuous villas. As they had the power and the arms in their hands, the peaceful and the industrious had no alternative but to submit. They went on as well as they could with their labors, bearing patiently every interruption, returning again to till their fields after the desolating march of the army had passed away, and repairing the injuries of violence, and the losses sustained by plunder, without useless repining. They looked upon an armed government as a necessary and inevitable affliction of humanity, and submitted to its destructive violence as they would submit to an earthquake or a pestilence. The tillers of the soil manage better in this country at the present day. They have the power in their own hands, and they watch very narrowly to prevent the organization of such hordes of armed desperadoes as have held the peaceful inhabitants of Europe in terror from the earliest periods down to the present day.

Julius Caesar.

Sylla's animosity against him.

Caesar refuses to repudiate his wife.

His flight.

When Sylla returned to Rome, and took possession of the supreme power there, in looking over the lists of public men, there was one whom he did not know, at first what to do with. It was the young Julius Caesar, the subject of this history. Caesar was, by birth, patrician, having descended from a long line of noble ancestors. There had been, before his day, a great many Caesars who had held the highest offices of the state, and many of them had been celebrated in history. He naturally, therefore, belonged to Sylla's side, as Sylla was the representative of the patrician interest. But then Caesar had personally been inclined toward the party of Marius. The elder Marius had married his aunt, and, besides, Caesar himself had married the daughter of Cinna, who had been the most efficient and powerful of Marius's coadjutors and friends. Caesar was at this time a very young man, and he was of an ardent and reckless character, though he had, thus far, taken no active part in public affairs. Sylla overlooked him for a time, but at length was about to put his name on the list of the proscribed. Some of the nobles, who were friends both of Sylla and of Caesar too, interceded for the young man; Sylla yielded to their request, or, rather, suspended his decision, and sent orders to Caesar to repudiate his wife, the daughter of Cinna. Her name was Cornelia. Caesar absolutely refused to repudiate his wife. He was influenced in this decision partly by affection for Cornelia, and partly by a sort of stern and indomitable insubmissiveness, which formed, from his earliest years, a prominent trait in his character, and which led him, during all his life, to brave every possible danger rather than allow himself to be controlled. Caesar knew very well that, when this his refusal should be reported to Sylla, the next order would be for his destruction. He accordingly fled. Sylla deprived him of his titles and offices, confiscated his wife's fortune and his own patrimonial estate, and put his name upon the list of the public enemies. Thus Caesar became a fugitive and an exile. The adventures which befell him in his wanderings will be described in the following chapter.

Sylla made dictator.

He resigns his power.

Sylla was now in the possession of absolute power. He was master of Rome, and of all the countries over which Rome held sway. Still he was nominally not a magistrate, but only a general returning victoriously from his Asiatic campaign, and putting to death, somewhat irregularly, it is true, by a sort of martial law persons whom he found, as he said, disturbing the public peace. After having thus effectually disposed of the power of his enemies, he laid aside, ostensibly, the government of the sword, and submitted himself and his future measures to the control of law. He placed himself ostensibly at the disposition of the city. They chose him dictator, which was investing him with absolute and unlimited power. He remained on this, the highest pinnacle of worldly ambition, a short time, and then resigned his power, and devoted the remainder of his days to literary pursuits and pleasures. Monster as he was in the cruelties which he inflicted upon his political foes, he was intellectually of a refined and cultivated mind, and felt an ardent interest in the promotion of literature and the arts.

Opinion of mankind in regard to Marius and Sylla.

The quarrel between Marius and Sylla, in respect to every thing which can make such a contest great, stands in the estimation of mankind as the greatest personal quarrel which the history of the world has ever recorded. Its origin was in the simple personal rivalry of two ambitious men. It involved, in its consequences, the peace and happiness of the world. In their reckless struggles, the fierce combatants trampled on every thing that came in their way, and destroyed mercilessly, each in his turn, all that opposed them. Mankind have always execrated their crimes, but have never ceased to admire the frightful and almost superhuman energy with which they committed them.

## CHAPTER II.: CAESAR'S EARLY YEARS.

Caesar's resolution.

Caesar does not seem to have been much disheartened and depressed by his misfortunes. He possessed in his early life more than the usual share of buoyancy and light-heartedness of youth, and he went away from Rome to enter, perhaps, upon years of exile and wandering, with a determination to face boldly and to brave the evils and dangers which surrounded him, and not to succumb to them.

His person and character.

Sometimes they who become great in their maturer years are thoughtful, grave, and sedate when young. It was not so, however, with Caesar. He was of a very gay and lively disposition. He was tall and handsome in his person, fascinating in his manners, and fond of society, as people always are who know or who suppose that they shine in it. He had seemed, in a word, during his residence at Rome, wholly intent upon the pleasures of a gay and joyous life, and upon the personal observation which his rank, his wealth, his agreeable manners and his position in society secured for him. In fact, they who observed and studied his character in these early years, thought that, although his situation was very favorable for acquiring power and renown, he would never feel any strong degree of ambition to avail himself of its advantages. He was too much interested, they thought, in personal pleasures ever to become great, either as a military commander or a statesman.

Sylla's estimation of Caesar.

Caesar's friends intercede for him.

Sylla, however, thought differently. He had penetration enough to perceive, beneath all the gayety and love of pleasure which characterized Caesar's youthful life, the germs of a sterner and more aspiring spirit, which, he was very sorry to see, was likely to expend its future energies in hostility to him. By refusing to submit to Sylla's commands, Caesar had, in effect, thrown himself entirely upon the other party, and would be, of course, in future identified with them. Sylla consequently looked upon him now as a confirmed and settled enemy. Some friends of Caesar among the patrician families interceded in his behalf with Sylla again, after he had fled from Rome. They wished Sylla to pardon him, saying that he was a mere boy and could do him no harm. Sylla shook his head, saying that, young as he was, he saw in him indications of a future power which he thought was more to be dreaded than that of many Mariuses.

Caesar's studies.

His ambition to be an orator.

One reason which led Sylla to form this opinion of Caesar was, that the young nobleman, with all his love of gayety and pleasure, had not neglected his studies, but had taken great pains to perfect himself in such intellectual pursuits as ambitious men who looked forward to political influence and ascendency were accustomed to prosecute in those days He had studied the Greek language, and read the works of Greek historians; and he attended lectures on philosophy and rhetoric, and was obviously interested deeply in acquiring power as a public speaker. To write and speak well gave a public man great influence in those days. Many of the measures of the government were determined by the action of great assemblies of the free citizens, which action was itself, in a great measure, controlled by the harangues of orators who had such powers of voice and such qualities of mind as enabled them to gain the attention and sway the opinions of large bodies of men.

The Forum.

Its porticoes and statues.

Attractions of the Forum.

It most not be supposed, however, that this popular power was shared by all the inhabitants of the city. At one time, when the population of the city was about three millions the number of free citizens was only three hundred thousand. The rest were laborers, artisans, and slaves, who had no voice in public affairs. The free citizens held very frequent public assemblies. There were various squares and open spaces in the city where such assemblies were convened, and where courts of justice were held. The Roman name for such a square was forum. There was one which was distinguished above all the rest, and was called emphatically The Forum. It was a magnificent square, surrounded by splendid edifices, and ornamented by sculptures and statues without number. There were ranges of porticoes along the sides, where the people were sheltered from the weather when necessary, though it is seldom that there is any necessity for shelter under an Italian sky. In this area and under these porticoes the people held their assemblies, and here courts of justice were accustomed to sit. The Forum was ornamented continually with new monuments, temples, statues, and columns by successful generals returning in triumph from foreign campaigns, and by proconsuls and praetors coming back enriched from their provinces, until it was fairly choked up with its architectural magnificence, and it had at last to be partially cleared again, as one would thin out too dense a forest, in order to make room for the assemblies which it was its main function to contain.

A ROMAN FORUM.

Harangues and political discussions.

The people of Rome had, of course, no printed books, and yet they were mentally cultivated and refined, and were qualified for a very high appreciation of intellectual pursuits and pleasures. In the absence, therefore, of all facilities for private reading, the Forum became the great central point of attraction. The same kind of interest which, in our day, finds its gratification in reading volumes of printed history quietly at home, or in silently perusing the columns of newspapers and magazines in libraries and reading-rooms, where a whisper is seldom heard, in Caesar's day brought every body to the Forum, to listen to historical harangues, or political discussions, or forensic arguments in the midst of noisy crowds. Here all tidings centered; here all questions were discussed and all great elections held. Here were waged those ceaseless conflicts of ambition and struggles of power on which the fate of nations, and sometimes the welfare of almost half mankind depended. Of course, every ambitious man who aspired to an ascendency over his fellow-men, wished to make his voice heard in the Forum. To calm the boisterous tumult there, and to hold, as some of the Roman orators could do, the vast assemblies in silent and breathless attention, was a power as delightful in its exercise as it was glorious in its fame. Caesar had felt this ambition, and had devoted himself very earnestly to the study of oratory.

Apollonius.

Caesar studies under him.

His teacher was Apollonius, a philosopher and rhetorician from Rhodes. Rhodes is a Grecian island, near the southwestern coast of Asia Minor Apollonius was a teacher of great celebrity, and Caesar became a very able writer and speaker under his instructions. His time and attention were, in fact, strangely divided between the highest and noblest intellectual avocations, and the lowest sensual pleasures of a gay and dissipated life. The coming of Sylla had, however, interrupted all; and, after receiving the dictator's command to give up his wife and abandon the Marian faction, and determining to disobey it, he fled suddenly from Rome, as was stated at the close of the last chapter, at midnight, and in disguise.

Caesar's wanderings.

He is seized by a centurion.

He was sick, too, at the time, with an intermittent fever. The paroxysm returned once in three or four days, leaving him in tolerable health during the interval. He went first into the country of the Sabines, northeast of Rome, where he wandered up and down, exposed continually to great dangers from those who knew that he was an object of the great dictator's displeasure, and who were sure of favor and of a reward if they could carry his head to Sylla He had to change his quarters every day, and to resort to every possible mode of concealment. He was, however, at last discovered, and seized by a centurion. A centurion was a commander of a hundred men; his rank and his position therefore, corresponded somewhat with those of a captain in a modern army. Caesar was not much disturbed at this accident. He offered the centurion a bribe sufficient to induce him to give up his prisoner, and so escaped.

Caesar in Asia Minor.

He joins the court of Nicomedes.

The two ancient historians, whose records contain nearly all the particulars of the early life of Caesar which are now known, give somewhat contradictory accounts of the adventures which befell him during his subsequent wanderings. They relate, in general, the same incidents, but in such different connections, that the precise chronological order of the events which occurred can not now be ascertained. At all events, Caesar, finding that he was no longer safe in the vicinity of Rome, moved gradually to the eastward, attended by a few followers, until he reached the sea, and there he embarked on board a ship to leave his native land altogether. After various adventures and wanderings, he found himself at length in Asia Minor, and he made his way at last to the kingdom of Bithynia, on the northern shore. The name of the king of Bithynia was Nicomedes. Caesar joined himself to Nicomedes's court, and entered into his service. In the mean time, Sylla had ceased to pursue him, and ultimately granted him a pardon, but whether before or after this time is not now to be ascertained. At all events, Caesar became interested in the scenes and enjoyments of Nicomedes's court, and allowed the time to pass away without forming any plans for returning to Rome.

Cilicia.

Character of its inhabitants.

On the opposite side of Asia Minor, that is, on the southern shore, there was a wild and mountainous region called Cilicia. The great chain of mountains called Taurus approaches here very near to the sea, and the steep conformations of the land, which, in the interior, produce lofty ranges and summits, and dark valleys and ravines, form, along the line of the shore, capes and promontories, bounded by precipitous sides, and with deep bays and harbors between them. The people of Cilicia were accordingly half sailors, half mountaineers. They built swift galleys, and made excursions in great force over the Mediterranean Sea for conquest and plunder. They would capture single ships, and sometimes even whole fleets of merchantmen. They were even strong enough on many occasions to land and take possession of a harbor and a town, and hold it, often, for a considerable time, against all the efforts of the neighboring powers to dislodge them. In case, however, their enemies became at any time too strong for them, they would retreat to their harbors, which were so defended by the fortresses which guarded them, and by the desperate bravery of the garrisons, that the pursuers generally did not dare to attempt to force their way in; and if, in any case, a town or a port was taken, the indomitable savages would continue their retreat to the fastnesses of the mountains, where it was utterly useless to attempt to follow them.

The Cilicians wanting in poets and historians.

Robbers and pirates.

But with all their prowess and skill as naval combatants, and their hardihood as mountaineers, the Cilicians lacked one thing which is very essential in every nation to an honorable military fame. They had no poets or historians of their own, so that the story of their deeds had to be told to posterity by their enemies. If they had been able to narrate their own exploits, they would have figured, perhaps, upon the page of history as a small but brave and efficient maritime power, pursuing for many years a glorious career of conquest, and acquiring imperishable renown by their enterprise and success. As it was, the Romans, their enemies, described their deeds and gave them their designation. They called them robbers and pirates; and robbers and pirates they must forever remain.

Depredations of the Cilicians.

And it is, in fact, very likely true that the Cilician commanders did not pursue their conquests and commit their depredations on the rights and the property of others in quite so systematic and methodical a manner as some other conquering states have done. They probably seized private property a little more unceremoniously than is customary; though all belligerent nations, even in these Christian ages of the world, feel at liberty to seize and confiscate private property when they find it afloat at sea, while, by a strange inconsistency, they respect it on the land. The Cilician pirates considered themselves at war with all mankind, and, whatever merchandise they found passing from port to port along the shores of the Mediterranean, they considered lawful spoil. They intercepted the corn which was going from Sicily to Rome, and filled their own granaries with it. They got rich merchandise from the ships of Alexandria, which brought, sometimes, gold, and gems, and costly fabrics from the East; and they obtained, often, large sums of money by seizing men of distinction and wealth, who were continually passing to and fro between Italy and Greece, and holding them for a ransom. They were particularly pleased to get possession in this way of Roman generals and officers of state, who were going out to take the command of armies, or who were returning from their provinces with the wealth which they had accumulated there.

Expeditions sent against them.

Boldness and courage of the Cilicians.

Many expeditions were fitted out and many naval commanders were commissioned to suppress and subdue these common enemies of mankind, as the Romans called them. At one time, while a distinguished general, named Antonius, was in pursuit of them at the head of a fleet, a party of the pirates made a descent upon the Italian coast, south of Rome, at Nicenum, where the ancient patrimonial mansion of this very Antonius was situated, and took away several members of his family as captives, and so compelled him to ransom them by paying a very large sum of money. The pirates grew bolder and bolder in proportion to their success. They finally almost stopped all intercourse between Italy and Greece, neither the merchants daring to expose their merchandise, nor the passengers their persons to such dangers. They then approached nearer and nearer to Rome, and at last actually entered the Tiber, and surprised and carried off a Roman fleet which was anchored there. Caesar himself fell into the hands of these pirates at some time during the period of his wanderings.

They capture Caesar.

The pirates captured the ship in which he was sailing near Pharmacusa, a small island in the northeastern part of the Aegean Sea. He was not at this time in the destitute condition in which he had found himself on leaving Rome, but was traveling with attendants suitable to his rank, and in such a style and manner as at once made it evident to the pirates that he was a man of distinction. They accordingly held him for ransom, and, in the mean time, until he could take measures for raising the money, they kept him a prisoner on board the vessel which had captured him.

Caesar's air of superiority.

His ransom.

In this situation, Caesar, though entirely in the power and at the mercy of his lawless captors, assumed such an air of superiority and command in all his intercourse with them as at first awakened their astonishment, then excited their admiration, and ended in almost subjecting them to his will. He asked them what they demanded for his ransom. They said twenty talents, which was quite a large amount, a talent itself being a considerable sum of money. Caesar laughed at this demand, and told them it was plain that they did not know who he was, He would give them fifty talents. He then sent away his attendants to the shore, with orders to proceed to certain cities where he was known, in order to procure the money, retaining only a physician and two servants for himself. While his messengers were gone, he remained on board the ship of his captors, assuming in every respect the air and manner of their master. When he wished to sleep, if they made a noise which disturbed him, he sent them orders to be still. He joined them in their sports and diversions on the deck, surpassing them in their feats, and taking the direction of every thing as if he were their acknowledged leader. He wrote orations and verses which he read to them, and if his wild auditors did not appear to appreciate the literary excellence of his compositions, he told them that they were stupid fools without any taste, adding, by way of apology, that nothing better could be expected of such barbarians.

The pirates asked him one day what he should do to them if he should ever, at any future time, take them prisoners. Caesar said that he would crucify every one of them.

Caesar at liberty.

He captures the pirates in his turn.

The ransom money at length arrived. Caesar paid it to the pirates, and they, faithful to their covenant, sent him in a boat to the land. He was put ashore on the coast of Asia Minor. He proceeded immediately to Miletus, the nearest port, equipped a small fleet there, and put to sea. He sailed at once to the roadstead where the pirates had been lying, and found them still at anchor there, in perfect security. He attacked them, seized their ships, recovered his ransom money, and took the men all prisoners. He conveyed his captives to the land, and there fulfilled his threat that he would crucify them by cutting their throats and nailing their dead bodies to crosses which his men erected for the purpose along the shore.

Caesar at Rhodes.

During his absence from Rome Caesar went to Rhodes, where his former preceptor resided, and he continued to pursue there for some time his former studies. He looked forward still to appearing one day in the Roman Forum. In fact, he began to receive messages from his friends at home that they thought it would be safe for him to return. Sylla had gradually withdrawn from power, and finally had died. The aristocratical party were indeed still in the ascendency, but the party of Marius had begun to recover a little from the total overthrow with which Sylla's return, and his terrible military vengeance, had overwhelmed them. Caesar himself, therefore, they thought, might, with prudent management, be safe in returning to Rome.

He returns to Rome.

Caesar impeaches Dolabella.

Excitement in consequence.

He returned, but not to be prudent or cautious; there was no element of prudence or caution in his character. As soon as he arrived, he openly espoused the popular party. His first public act was to arraign the governor of the great province of Macedonia, through which he had passed on his way to Bithynia. It was a consul whom he thus impeached, and a strong partisan of Sylla's. His name was Dolabella. The people were astonished at his daring in thus raising the standard of resistance to Sylla's power, indirectly, it is true, but none the less really on that account. When the trial came on, and Caesar appeared at the Forum, he gained great applause by the vigor and force of his oratory. There was, of course, a very strong and general interest felt in the case; the people all seeming to understand that, in this attack on Dolabella, Caesar was appearing as their champion, and their hopes were revived at having at last found a leader capable of succeeding

Marius, and building up their cause again. Dolabella was ably defended by orators on the other side, and was, of course, acquitted, for the power of Sylla's party was still supreme. All Rome, however, was aroused and excited by the boldness of Caesar's attack, and by the extraordinary ability which he evinced in his mode of conducting it. He became, in fact, at once one of the most conspicuous and prominent men in the city.

Caesar's increasing power.

Encouraged by his success, and the applauses which he received, and feeling every day a greater and greater consciousness of power, he began to assume more and more openly the character of the leader of the popular party. He devoted himself to public speaking in the Forum, both before popular assemblies and in the courts of justice, where he was employed a great deal as an advocate to defend those who were accused of political crimes. The people, considering him as their rising champion, were predisposed to regard every thing that he did with favor, and there was really a great intellectual power displayed in his orations and harangues. He acquired, in a word, great celebrity by his boldness and energy, and his boldness and energy were themselves increased in their turn as he felt the strength of his position increase with his growing celebrity.

Death of Marius's wife.

Caesar's panegyric on Marius's wife.

Its success.

At length the wife of Marius, who was Caesar's aunt, died. She had lived in obscurity since her husband's proscription and death, his party having been put down so effectually that it was dangerous to appear to be her friend. Caesar, however, made preparations for a magnificent funeral for her. There was a place in the Forum, a sort of pulpit, where public orators were accustomed to stand in addressing the assembly on great occasions. This pulpit was adorned with the brazen beaks of ships which had been taken by the Romans in former wars The name of such a beak was rostrum; in the plural, rostra. The pulpit was itself, therefore, called the Rostra, that is, The Beaks; and the people were addressed from it on great public occasions. Caesar pronounced a splendid panegyric upon the wife of Marius, at this her funeral, from the Rostra, in the presence of a vast concourse of spectators, and he had the boldness to bring out and display to the people certain household images of Marius, which had been concealed from view ever since his death. Producing them again on such an occasion was annulling, so far as a public orator could do it, the sentence of condemnation which Sylla and the patrician party had pronounced against him, and bringing him forward again as entitled to public admiration and applause. The patrician partisans who were present attempted to rebuke this bold maneuver with expressions of disapprobation, but these expressions were drowned in the loud and long-continued bursts of applause with which the great mass of the assembled multitude hailed and sanctioned it. The experiment was very bold and very hazardous, but it was triumphantly successful.

Caesar's oration on his wife.

Alarm of the patricians.

A short time after this Caesar had another opportunity for delivering a funeral oration; it was in the case of his own wife, the daughter of Cinna, who had been the colleague and coadjutor of Marius during the days of his power. It was not usual to pronounce such panegyrics upon Roman ladies unless they had attained to an advanced age. Caesar, however, was disposed to make the case of his own wife an exception to the ordinary rule. He saw in the occasion an opportunity to give a new impulse to the popular cause, and to make further progress in gaining the popular favor. The experiment was successful in this instance too. The people were pleased at the apparent affection which his action evinced; and as Cornelia was the daughter of Cinna, he had opportunity, under pretext of praising the birth and parentage of the deceased, to laud the men whom Sylla's party had outlawed and destroyed. In a word, the patrician party saw with anxiety and dread that Caesar was rapidly consolidating and organizing, and bringing back to its pristine strength and vigor, a party whose restoration to power would of course involve their own political, and perhaps personal ruin.

Caesar in office.

Shows and entertainments.

Caesar began soon to receive appointments to public office, and thus rapidly increased his influence and power. Public officers and candidates for office were accustomed in those days to expend great sums of money in shows and spectacles to amuse the people. Caesar went beyond all limits in these expenditures. He brought gladiators from distant provinces, and trained them at great expense, to fight in the enormous amphitheaters of the city, in the midst of vast assemblies of men. Wild beasts were procured also from the forests of Africa, and brought over in great numbers, under his direction, that the people might be entertained by their combats with captives taken in war, who were reserved for this dreadful fate. Caesar gave, also, splendid entertainments, of the most luxurious and costly character, and he mingled with his guests at these entertainments, and with the people at large on other occasions, in so complaisant and courteous a manner as to gain universal favor.

Caesar's extravagances.

His embarrassments.

He soon, by these means, not only exhausted all his own pecuniary resources, but plunged himself enormously into debt. It was not difficult for such a man in those days to procure an almost unlimited credit for such purposes as these, for every one knew that, if he finally succeeded in placing himself, by means of the popularity thus acquired, in stations of power, he could soon indemnify himself and all others who had aided him. The peaceful merchants, and artisans, and husbandmen of the distant provinces over which he expected to rule, would yield the revenues necessary to fill the treasuries thus exhausted. Still, Caesar's expenditures were so lavish, and the debts he incurred were so enormous, that those who had not the most unbounded confidence in his capacity and his powers believed him irretrievably ruined.

The particulars, however, of these difficulties, and the manner in which Caesar contrived to extricate himself from them, will be more fully detailed in the next chapter.

## CHAPTER III.: ADVANCEMENT TO THE CONSULSHIP.

Caesar's rise to power.

From this time, which was about sixty-seven years before the birth of Christ, Caesar remained for nine years generally at Rome, engaged there in a constant struggle for power. He was successful in these efforts, rising all the time from one position of influence and honor to another, until he became altogether the most prominent and powerful man in the city. A great many incidents are recorded, as attending these contests, which illustrate in a very striking manner the strange mixture of rude violence and legal formality by which Rome was in those days governed.

Government of Rome.

Bribery and corruption.

Public amusements.

Many of the most important offices of the state depended upon the votes of the people; and as the people had very little opportunity to become acquainted with the real merits of the case in respect to questions of government, they gave their votes very much according to the personal popularity of the candidate. Public men had very little moral principle in those days, and they would accordingly resort to any means whatever to procure this personal popularity. They who wanted office were accustomed to bribe influential men among the people to support them, sometimes by promising them subordinate offices, and sometimes by the direct donation of sums of money; and they would try to please the mass of the people, who were too numerous to be paid with offices or with gold, by shows and spectacles, and entertainments of every kind which they would provide for their amusement.

This practice seems to us very absurd; and we wonder that the Roman people should tolerate it, since it is evident that the means for defraying these expenses must come, ultimately, in some way or other, from them. And yet, absurd as it seems, this sort of policy is not wholly disused even in our day. The operas and the theaters, and other similar establishments in France, are sustained, in part, by the government; and the liberality and efficiency with which this is done, forms, in some degree, the basis of the popularity of each succeeding administration. The plan is better systematized and regulated in our day, but it is, in its nature, substantially the same.

Amusements for the people.

In fact, furnishing amusements for the people, and also providing supplies for their wants, as well as affording them protection, were considered the legitimate objects of government in those days. It is very different at the present time, and especially in this country. The whole community are now united in the desire to confine the functions of government within the narrowest possible limits, such as to include only the preservation of public order and public safety. The people prefer to supply their own wants and to provide their own enjoyments, rather than to invest government with the power to do it for them, knowing very well that, on the latter plan, the burdens they will have to bear, though concealed for a time, must be doubled in the end.

Provided by the government.

How the people were supported.

Agrarian laws.

It must not be forgotten, however, that there were some reasons in the days of the Romans for providing public amusements for the people on an extended scale which do not exist now. They had very few facilities then for the private and separate enjoyments of home, so that they were much more inclined than the people of this country are now to seek pleasure abroad and in public. The climate, too, mild and genial nearly all the year, favored this. Then they were not interested, as men are now, in the pursuits and avocations of private industry. The people of Rome were not a community of merchants, manufacturers, and citizens, enriching themselves, and adding to the comforts and enjoyments of the rest of mankind by the products of their labor. They were supported, in a great measure, by the proceeds of the tribute of foreign provinces, and by the plunder taken by the generals in the name of the state in foreign wars. From the same source, too--foreign conquest--captives were brought home, to be trained as gladiators to amuse them with their combats, and statues and paintings to ornament the public buildings of the city. In the same manner, large quantities of corn, which had been taken in the provinces, were often distributed at Rome. And sometimes even land itself, in large tracts, which had been confiscated by the state, or otherwise taken from the original possessors, was divided among the people. The laws enacted from time to time for this purpose were called Agrarian laws; and the phrase afterward passed into a sort of proverb, inasmuch as plans proposed in modern times for conciliating the favor of the populace by sharing among them property belonging to the state or to the rich, are designated by the name of Agrarianism.

Government of Rome.

Its foreign policy.

Thus Rome was a city supported, in a great measure, by the fruits of its conquests, that is, in a certain sense, by plunder. It was a vast community most efficiently and admirably organized for this purpose; and yet it would not be perfectly just to designate the people simply as a band of robbers. They rendered, in some sense, an equivalent for what they took, in establishing and enforcing a certain organization of society throughout the world, and in preserving a sort of public order and peace. They built cities, they constructed aqueducts and roads; they formed harbors, and protected them by piers and by castles; they protected commerce, and cultivated the arts, and encouraged literature, and enforced a general quiet and peace among mankind, allowing of no violence or war except what they themselves created. Thus they governed the world, and they felt, as all governors of mankind always do, fully entitled to supply themselves with the comforts and conveniences of life, in consideration of the service which they thus rendered.

Caesar's policy.

Of course, it was to be expected that they would sometimes quarrel among themselves about the spoils. Ambitious men were always arising, eager to obtain opportunities to make fresh conquests, and to bring home new supplies, and those who were most successful in making the results of their conquests available in adding to the wealth and to the public enjoyments of the city, would, of course, be most popular with the voters. Hence extortion in the provinces, and the most profuse and lavish expenditure in the city, became the policy which every great man must pursue to rise to power.

His success.

Caesar entered into this policy with his whole soul, founding all his hopes of success upon the favor of the populace. Of course, he had many rivals and opponents among the patrician ranks, and in the Senate, and they often impeded and thwarted his plans and measures for a time, though he always triumphed in the end.

He is made quaestor.

Caesar leaves Spain.

His project.

One of the first offices of importance to which he attained was that of quaestor, as it was called, which office called him away from Rome into the province of Spain, making him the second in command there. The officer first in command in the province was, in this instance, a praetor. During his absence in Spain, Caesar replenished in some degree his exhausted finances, but he soon became very much discontented with so subordinate a position. His discontent was greatly increased by his coming unexpectedly, one day, at a city then called Hades--the present Cadiz--upon a statue of Alexander, which adorned one of the public edifices there. Alexander died when he was only about thirty years of age, having before that period made himself master of the world. Caesar was himself now about thirty-five years of age, and it made him very sad to reflect that, though he had lived five years longer than Alexander, he had yet accomplished so little. He was thus far only the second in a province, while he burned with an insatiable ambition to be the first in Rome. The reflection made him so uneasy that he left his post before his time expired, and went back to Rome, forming, on the way, desperate projects for getting power there.

Caesar accused of treason.

His rivals and enemies accused him of various schemes, more or less violent and treasonable in their nature, but how justly it is not now possible to ascertain. They alleged that one of his plans was to join some of the neighboring colonies, whose inhabitants wished to be admitted to the freedom of the city, and, making common cause with them, to raise an armed force and take possession of Rome. It was said that, to prevent the accomplishment of this design, an army which they had raised for the purpose of an expedition against the Cilician pirates was detained from its march, and that Caesar, seeing that the government were on their guard against him, abandoned the plan.

They also charged him with having formed, after this, a plan within the city for assassinating the senators in the senate house, and then usurping, with his fellow-conspirators, the supreme power. Crassus, who was a man of vast wealth and a great friend of Caesar's, was associated with him in this plot, and was to have been made dictator if it had succeeded. But, notwithstanding the brilliant prize with which Caesar attempted to allure Crassus to the enterprise, his courage failed him when the time for action arrived. Courage and enterprise, in fact, ought not to be expected of the rich; they are the virtues of poverty.

He is made aedile.

Gladiatorial shows.

Caesar's increasing popularity.

Though the Senate were thus jealous and suspicious of Caesar, and were charging him continually with these criminal designs, the people were on his side; and the more he was hated by the great, the more strongly he became intrenched in the popular favor. They chose him aedile. The aedile had the charge of the public edifices of the city, and of the games spectacles, and shows which were exhibited in them. Caesar entered with great zeal into the discharge of the duties of this office. He made arrangements for the entertainment of the people on the most magnificent scale, and made great additions and improvements to the public buildings, constructing porticoes and piazzas around the areas where his gladiatorial shows and the combats with wild beasts were to be exhibited. He provided gladiators in such numbers, and organized and arranged them in such a manner, ostensibly for their training, that his enemies among the nobility pretended to believe that he was intending to use them as an armed force against the government of the city. They accordingly made laws limiting and restricting the number of the gladiators to be employed. Caesar then exhibited his shows on the reduced scale which the new laws required, taking care that the people should understand to whom the responsibility for this reduction in the scale of their pleasures belonged. They, of course, murmured against the Senate, and Caesar stood higher in their favor than ever.

Caesar thwarted.

His resentment.

The statutes of Marius restored.

Rage of the patricians.

He was getting, however, by these means, very deeply involved in debt; and, in order partly to retrieve his fortunes in this respect, he made an attempt to have Egypt assigned to him as a province. Egypt was then an immensely rich and fertile country. It had, however, never been a Roman province. It was an independent kingdom, in alliance with the Romans, and Caesar's proposal that it should be assigned to him as a province appeared very extraordinary. His pretext was, that the people of Egypt had recently deposed and expelled their king, and that, consequently, the Romans might properly take possession of it. The Senate, however, resisted this plan, either from jealousy of Caesar or from a sense of justice to Egypt; and, after a violent contest, Caesar found himself compelled to give up the design. He felt, however, a strong degree of resentment against the patrician party who had thus thwarted his designs. Accordingly, in order to avenge himself upon them, he one night replaced certain statues and trophies of Marius in the Capitol, which had been taken down by order of Sylla when he returned to power. Marius, as will be recollected, had been the great champion of the popular party, and the enemy of the patricians; and, at the time of his down-fall, all the memorials of his power and greatness had been every where removed from Rome, and among them these statues and trophies, which had been erected in the Capitol in commemoration of some former victories, and had remained there until Sylla's triumph, when they were taken down and destroyed. Caesar now ordered new ones to be made, far more magnificent than before. They were made secretly, and put up in the night.

His office as aedile gave him the necessary authority. The next morning, when the people saw these splendid monuments of their great favorite restored, the whole city was animated with excitement and joy. The patricians, on the other hand, were filled with vexation and rage. "Here is a single officer," said they, "who is attempting to restore, by his individual authority, what has been formally abolished by a decree of the Senate. He is trying to see how much we will bear. If he finds that we will submit to this, he will attempt bolder measures still." They accordingly commenced a movement to have the statues and trophies taken down again, but the people rallied in vast numbers in defense of them. They made the Capitol ring with their shouts of applause; and the Senate, finding their power insufficient to cope with so great a force, gave up the point, and Caesar gained the day.

The Good Goddess.

Caesar had married another wife after the death of Cornelia. Her name was Pompeia, He divorced Pompeia about this time, under very extraordinary circumstances. Among the other strange religious ceremonies and celebrations which were observed in those days, was one called the celebration of the mysteries of the Good Goddess. This celebration was held by females alone, every thing masculine being most carefully excluded. Even the pictures of men, if there were any upon the walls of the house where the assembly was held, were covered. The persons engaged spent the night together in music and dancing and various secret ceremonies, half pleasure, half worship, according to the ideas and customs of the time.

Clodius.

Caesar divorces his wife.

The mysteries of the Good Goddess were to be celebrated one night at Caesar's house, he himself having, of course, withdrawn. In the middle of the night, the whole company in one of the apartments were thrown into consternation at finding that one of their number was a man. He had a smooth and youthful-looking face, and was very perfectly disguised in the dress of a female. He proved to be a certain Clodius, a very base and dissolute young man, though of great wealth and high connections. He had been admitted by a female slave of Pompeia's, whom he had succeeded in bribing. It was suspected that it was with Pompeia's concurrence. At any rate, Caesar immediately divorced his wife. The Senate ordered an inquiry into the affair, and, after the other members of the household had given their testimony, Caesar himself was called upon, but he had nothing to say. He knew nothing about it. They asked him, then, why he had divorced Pompeia, unless he had some evidence for believing her guilty, He replied, that a wife of Caesar must not only be without crime, but without suspicion.

Quarrel of Clodius and Milo.

Violence of the time.

Clodius was a very desperate and lawless character, and his subsequent history shows, in a striking point of view, the degree of violence and disorder which reigned in those times. He became involved in a bitter contention with another citizen whose name was Milo, and each, gaining as many adherents as he could, at length drew almost the whole city into their quarrel. Whenever they went out, they were attended with armed bands, which were continually in danger of coming into collision. The collision at last came, quite a battle was fought, and Clodius was killed. This made the difficulty worse than it was before. Parties were formed, and violent disputes arose on the question of bringing Milo to trial for the alleged murder. He was brought to trial at last, but so great was the public excitement, that the consuls for the time surrounded and filled the whole Forum with armed men while the trial was proceeding, to ensure the safety of the court.

Conspiracy of Catiline.

Warm debate in the Senate.

Caesar in danger of violence.

In fact, violence mingled itself continually, in those times, with almost all public proceedings, whenever any special combination of circumstances occurred to awaken unusual excitement. At one time, when Caesar was in office, a very dangerous conspiracy was brought to light, which was headed by the notorious Catiline. It was directed chiefly against the Senate and the higher departments of the government; it contemplated, in fact, their utter destruction, and the establishment of an entirely new government on the ruins of the existing constitution. Caesar was himself accused of a participation in this plot. When it was discovered, Catiline himself fled; some of the other conspirators were, however, arrested, and there was a long and very excited debate in the Senate on the question of their punishment. Some were for death. Caesar, however, very earnestly opposed this plan, recommending, instead, the confiscation of the estates of the conspirators, and their imprisonment in some of the distant cities of Italy. The dispute grew very warm, Caesar urging his point with great perseverance and determination, and with a degree of violence which threatened seriously to obstruct the proceedings, when a body of armed men, a sort of guard of honor stationed there, gathered around him, and threatened him with their swords. Quite a scene of disorder and terror ensued. Some of the senators arose hastily and fled from the vicinity of Caesar's seat to avoid the danger. Others, more courageous, or more devoted in their attachment to him, gathered around him to protect him, as far as they could, by interposing their bodies between his person and the weapons of his assailants. Caesar soon left the Senate, and for a long time would return to it no more.

Caesar's struggle for the office of pontifex maximus.

Although Caesar was all this time, on the whole, rising in influence and power, there were still fluctuations in his fortune, and the tide sometimes, for a short period, went strongly against him. He was at one time, when greatly involved in debt, and embarrassed in all his affairs, a candidate for a very high office, that of Pontifex Maximus, or sovereign pontiff. The office of the pontifex was originally that of building and keeping custody of the bridges of the city, the name being derived from the Latin word pons, which signifies bridge. To this, however, had afterward been added the care of the temples, and finally the regulation and control of the ceremonies of religion, so that it came in the end to be an office of the highest dignity and honor. Caesar made the most desperate efforts to secure his election, resorting to such measures, expending such sums, and involving himself in debt to such an extreme, that, if he failed, he would be irretrievably ruined. His mother, sympathizing with him in his anxiety, kissed him when he went away from the house on the morning of the election, and bade hem farewell with tears. He told her that he should come home that night the pontiff, or he should never come home at all. He succeeded in gaining the election.

He is deposed.

Caesar's forbearance.

He is restored to office.

At one time Caesar was actually deposed from a high office which he held, by a decree of the Senate. He determined to disregard this decree, and go on in the discharge of his office as usual. But the Senate, whose ascendency was now, for some reason, once more established, prepared to prevent him by force of arms. Caesar, finding that he was not sustained, gave up the contest, put off his robes of office, and went home. Two days afterward a reaction occurred. A mass of the populace came together to his house, and offered their assistance to restore his rights and vindicate his honor. Caesar, however, contrary to what every one would have expected of him, exerted his influence to calm and quiet the mob, and then sent them away, remaining himself in private as before. The Senate had been alarmed at the first outbreak of the tumult, and a meeting had been suddenly convened to consider what measures to adopt in such a crisis. When, however, they found that Caesar had himself interposed, and by his own personal influence had saved the city from the danger which threatened it, they were so strongly impressed with a sense of his forbearance and generosity, that they sent for him to come to the senate house, and, after formally expressing their thanks, they canceled their former vote, and restored him to his office again. This change in the action of the Senate does not, however, necessarily indicate so great a change of individual sentiment as one might at first imagine. There was, undoubtedly, a large minority who were averse to his being deposed in the first instance but, being outvoted, the decree of deposition was passed. Others were, perhaps, more or less doubtful. Caesar's generous forbearance in refusing the offered aid of the populace carried over a number of these sufficient to shift the majority, and thus the action of the body was reversed. It is in this way that the sudden and apparently total changes in the action of deliberative assemblies which often take place, and which would otherwise, in some cases, be almost incredible, are to be explained.

Caesar implicated in Catiline's conspiracy.

He arrests Vettius.

After this, Caesar became involved in another difficulty, in consequence of the appearance of some definite and positive evidence that he was connected with Catiline in his famous conspiracy. One of the senators said that Catiline himself had informed him that Caesar was one of the accomplices of the plot. Another witness, named Vettius, laid an information against Caesar before a Roman magistrate, and offered to produce Caesar's handwriting in proof of his participation in the conspirator's designs Caesar was very much incensed, and his manner of vindicating himself from these serious charges was as singular as many of his other deeds. He arrested Vettius, and sentenced him to pay a heavy fine, and to be imprisoned; and he contrived also to expose him, in the course of the proceedings, to the mob in the Forum, who were always ready to espouse Caesar's cause, and who, on this occasion, beat Vettius so unmercifully, that he barely escaped with his life. The magistrate, too, was thrown into prison for having dared to take an information against a superior officer.

Caesar's embarrassment.

Spain is assigned to him.

At last Caesar became so much involved in debt, through the boundless extravagance of his expenditures, that something must be done to replenish his exhausted finances. He had, however, by this time, risen so high in official influence and power, that he succeeded in having Spain assigned to him as his province, and he began to make preparations to proceed to it. His creditors, however, interposed, unwilling to let him go without giving them security. In this dilemma, Caesar succeeded in making an arrangement with Crassus, who has already been spoken of as a man of unbounded wealth and great ambition, but not possessed of any considerable degree of intellectual power. Crassus consented to give the necessary security, with an understanding that Caesar was to repay him by exerting his political influence in his favor. So soon as this arrangement was made, Caesar set off in a sudden and private manner, as if he expected that otherwise some new difficulty would intervene.

The Swiss hamlet.

He went to Spain by land, passing through Switzerland on the way. He stopped with his attendants one night at a very insignificant village of shepherds' huts among the mountains. Struck with the poverty and worthlessness of all they saw in this wretched hamlet, Caesar's friends were wondering whether the jealousy, rivalry, and ambition which reigned among men every where else in the world could find any footing there, when Caesar told them that, for his part, he should rather choose to be first in such a village as that than the second at Rome. The story has been repeated a thousand times, and told to every successive generation now for nearly twenty centuries, as an illustration of the peculiar type and character of the ambition which controls such a soul as that of Caesar.

Caesar's ambition.

Caesar was very successful in the administration of his province; that is to say, he returned in a short time with considerable military glory, and with money enough to pay all his debts, and famish him with means for fresh electioneering.

Manner of choosing the consuls.

Pompey and Crassus.

He now felt strong enough to aspire to the office of consul, which was the highest office of the Roman state. When the line of kings had been deposed, the Romans had vested the supreme magistracy in the hands of two consuls, who were chosen annually in a general election, the formalities of which were all very carefully arranged. The current of popular opinion was, of course, in Caesar's favor, but he had many powerful rivals and enemies among the great, who, however, hated and opposed each other as well as him. There was at that time a very bitter feud between Pompey and Crassus, each of them struggling for power against the efforts of the other. Pompey possessed great influence through his splendid abilities and his military renown. Crassus, as has already been stated, was powerful through his wealth. Caesar, who had some influence with them both, now conceived the bold design of reconciling them, and then of availing himself of their united aid in accomplishing his own particular ends.

The first triumvirate.

He succeeded perfectly well in this management. He represented to them that, by contending against each other, they only exhausted their own powers, and strengthened the arms of their common enemies. He proposed to them to unite with one another and with him, and thus make common cause to promote their common interest and advancement. They willingly acceded to this plan, and a triple league was accordingly formed, in which they each bound themselves to promote, by every means in his power, the political elevation of the others, and not to take any public step or adopt any measures without the concurrence of the three. Caesar faithfully observed the obligations of this league so long as he could use his two associates to promote his own ends, and then he abandoned it.

Caesar a candidate for the consulship.

Having, however, completed this arrangement, he was now prepared to push vigorously his claims to be elected consul. He associated with his own name that of Lucceius, who was a man of great wealth, and who agreed to defray the expenses of the election for the sake of the honor of being consul with Caesar. Caesar's enemies, however, knowing that they probably could not prevent his election, determined to concentrate their strength in the effort to prevent his having the colleague he desired. They made choice, therefore, of a certain Bibulus as their candidate. Bibulus had always been a political opponent of Caesar's, and they thought that, by associating him with Caesar in the supreme magistracy, the pride and ambition of their great adversary might be held somewhat in check. They accordingly made a contribution among themselves to enable Bibulus to expend as much money in bribery as Lucceius, and the canvass went on.

Caesar assumes the whole power.

He imprisons Cato.

It resulted in the election of Caesar and Bibulus. They entered upon the duties of their office; but Caesar, almost entirely disregarding his colleague, began to assume the whole power, and proposed and carried measure after measure of the most extraordinary character, all aiming at the gratification of the populace. He was at first opposed violently both by Bibulus and by many leading members of the Senate, especially by Cato, a stern and inflexible patriot, whom neither fear of danger nor hope of reward could move from what he regarded his duty. But Caesar was now getting strong enough to put down the opposition which he encountered with out much scruple as to the means. He ordered Cato on one occasion to be arrested in the Senate and sent to prison. Another influential member of the Senate rose and was going out with him. Caesar asked him where he was going. He said he was going with Cato. He would rather, he said, be with Cato in prison, than in the Senate with Caesar.

Bibulus retires to his house.

The year of "Julius and Caesar."

Caesar treated Bibulus also with so much neglect, and assumed so entirely the whole control of the consular power, to the utter exclusion of his colleague, that Bibulus at last, completely discouraged and chagrined, abandoned all pretension to official authority, retired to his house, and shut himself up in perfect seclusion, leaving Caesar to his own way. It was customary among the Romans, in their historical and narrative writings, to designate the successive years, not by a numerical date as with us, but by the names of the consuls who held office in them. Thus, in the time of Caesar's consulship, the phrase would have been, "In the year of Caesar and Bibulus, consuls," according to the ordinary usage; but the wags of the city, in order to make sport of the assumptions of Caesar and the insignificance of Bibulus, used to say, "In the year of Julius and Caesar, consuls," rejecting the name of Bibulus altogether, and taking the two names of Caesar to make out the necessary duality.

## CHAPTER IV.: THE CONQUEST OF GAUL.

Caesar aspires to be a soldier.

His success and celebrity.

In attaining to the consulship, Caesar had reached the highest point of elevation which it was possible to reach as a mere citizen of Rome. His ambition was, however, of course, not satisfied. The only way to acquire higher distinction and to rise to higher power was to enter upon a career of foreign conquest. Caesar therefore aspired now to be a soldier. He accordingly obtained the command of an army, and entered upon a course of military campaigns in the heart of Europe, which he continued for eight years. These eight years constitute one of the most important and strongly-marked periods of his life. He was triumphantly successful in his military career, and he made, accordingly, a vast accession to his celebrity and power, in his own day, by the results of his campaigns. He also wrote, himself, an account of his adventures during this period, in which the events are recorded in so lucid and in so eloquent a manner, that the narrations have continued to be read by every successive generation of scholars down to the present day, and they have had a great influence in extending and perpetuating his fame.

Scenes of Caesar's exploits.

Cisalpine and Transalpine Gaul.

The principal scenes of the exploits which Caesar performed during the period of this his first great military career, were the north of Italy, Switzerland, France, Germany, and England, a great tract of country, nearly all of which he overran and conquered. A large portion of this territory was called Gaul in those days; the part on the Italian side of the Alps being named Cisalpine Gaul, while that which lay beyond was designated as Transalpine. Transalpine Gaul was substantially what is now France. There was a part of Transalpine Gaul which had been already conquered and reduced to a Roman province. It was called The Province then, and has retained the name, with a slight change in orthography, to the present day. It is now known as Provence.

Condition of Gaul in Caesar's day.

Singular cavalry.

The countries which Caesar went to invade were occupied by various nations and tribes, many of which were well organized and war-like, and some of them were considerably civilized and wealthy. They had extended tracts of cultivated land, the slopes of the hills and the mountain sides being formed into green pasturages, which were covered with flocks of goats, and sheep, and herds of cattle, while the smoother and more level tracts were adorned with smiling vineyards and broadly-extended fields of waving grain. They had cities, forts, ships, and armies. Their manners and customs would be considered somewhat rude by modern nations, and some of their usages of war were half barbarian. For example, in one of the nations which Caesar encountered, he found, as he says in his narrative, a corps of cavalry, as a constituent part of the army, in which, to every horse, there were two men, one the rider, and the other a sort of foot soldier and attendant. If the battle went against them, and the squadron were put to their speed in a retreat, these footmen would cling to the manes-of the horses, and then, half running, half flying, they would be borne along over the field, thus keeping always at the side of their comrades, and escaping with them to a place of safety.

Caesar's plans.

But, although the Romans were inclined to consider these nations as only half civilized, still there would be great glory, as Caesar thought, in subduing them, and probably great treasure would be secured in the conquest, both by the plunder and confiscation of governmental property, and by the tribute which would be collected in taxes from the people of the countries subdued. Caesar accordingly placed himself at the head of an army of three Roman legions, which he contrived, by means of a great deal of political maneuvering and management, to have raised and placed under his command. One of these legions, which was called the tenth legion, was his favorite corps, on account of the bravery and hardihood which they often displayed. At the head of these legions, Caesar set out for Gaul. He was at this time not far from forty years of age.

His pretexts.

Caesar had no difficulty in finding pretexts for making war upon any of these various nations that he might desire to subdue. They were, of course, frequently at war with each other, and there were at all times standing topics of controversy and unsettled disputes among them. Caesar had, therefore, only to draw near to the scene of contention, and then to take sides with one party or the other, it mattered little with which, for the affair almost always resulted, in the end, in his making himself master of both. The manner, however, in which this sort of operation was performed, can best be illustrated by an example, and we will take for the purpose the case of Ariovistus.

Ariovistus.

The Aeduans.

Ariovistus was a German king. He had been nominally a sort of ally of the Romans. He had extended his conquests across the Rhine into Gaul, and he held some nations there as his tributaries. Among these, the Aeduans were a prominent party, and, to simplify the account, we will take their name as the representative of all who were concerned. When Caesar came into the region of the Aeduans, he entered into some negotiations with them, in which they, as he alleges, asked his assistance to enable them to throw off the dominion of their German enemy. It is probable, in fact, that there was some proposition of this kind from them, for Caesar had abundant means of inducing them to make it, if he was disposed, and the receiving of such a communication furnished the most obvious and plausible pretext to authorize and justify his interposition.

Caesar accordingly sent a messenger across the Rhine to Ariovistus, saying that he wished to have an interview with him on business of importance, and asking him to name a time which would be convenient to him for the interview, and also to appoint some place in Gaul where he would attend.

Caesar's negotiations with Ariovistus.

To this Ariovistus replied, that if he had, himself, any business with Caesar, he would have waited upon him to propose it; and, in the same manner, if Caesar wished to see him, he must come into his own dominions. He said that it would not be safe for him to come into Gaul without an army, and that it was not convenient for him to raise and equip an army for such a purpose at that time.

His message.

Caesar sent again to Ariovistus to say, that since he was so unmindful of his obligations to the Roman people as to refuse an interview with him on business of common interest, he would state the particulars that he required of him. The Aeduans, he said, were now his allies, and under his protection; and Ariovistus must send back the hostages which he held from them, and bind himself henceforth not to send any more troops across the Rhine, nor make war upon the Aeduans, or injure them in any way. If he complied with these terms, all would be well. If he did not, Caesar said that he should not himself disregard the just complaints of his allies.

Ariovistus's spirited reply to Caesar.

Ariovistus had no fear of Caesar. Caesar had, in fact, thus far, not begun to acquire the military renown to which he afterward attained Ariovistus had, therefore, no particular cause to dread his power. He sent him back word that he did not understand why Caesar should interfere between him and his conquered province.

"The Aeduans," said he, "tried the fortune of war with me, and were overcome; and they must abide the issue. The Romans manage their conquered provinces as they judge proper, without holding themselves accountable to any one. I shall do the same with mine. All that I can say is, that so long as the Aeduans submit peaceably to my authority, and pay their tribute, I shall not molest them; as to your threat that you shall not disregard their complaints, you must know that no one has ever made war upon me but to his own destruction, and, if you wish to see how it will turn out in your case, you may make the experiment whenever you please."

Preparations for war.

Both parties immediately prepared for war. Ariovistus, instead of waiting to be attacked, assembled his army, crossed the Rhine, and advanced into the territories from which Caesar had undertaken to exclude him.

Panic in the Roman army.

As Caesar, however, began to make his arrangements for putting his army in motion to meet his approaching enemy, there began to circulate throughout the camp such extraordinary stories of the terrible strength and courage of the German soldiery as to produce a very general panic. So great, at length, became the anxiety and alarm, that even the officers were wholly dejected and discouraged; and as for the men, they were on the very eve of mutiny.

Caesar's address.

When Caesar understood this state of things, he called an assembly of the troops, and made an address to them. He told them that he was astonished to learn to what an extent an unworthy despondency and fear had taken possession of their minds, and how little confidence they reposed in him, their general. And then, after some further remarks about the duty of a soldier to be ready to go wherever his commander leads him, and presenting also some considerations in respect to the German troops with which they were going to contend, in order to show them that they had no cause to fear, he ended by saying that he had not been fully decided as to the time of marching, but that now he had concluded to give orders for setting out the next morning at three o'clock, that he might learn, as soon as possible, who were too cowardly to follow him. He would go himself, he said, if he was attended by the tenth legion alone He was sure that they would not shrink from any undertaking in which he led the way.

Effect of Caesar's address.

Proposals for an interview.

The soldiers, moved partly by shame, partly by the decisive and commanding tone which their general assumed, and partly reassured by the courage and confidence which he seemed to feel, laid aside their fears, and vied with each other henceforth in energy and ardor. The armies approached each other. Ariovistus sent to Caesar, saying that now, if he wished it, he was ready for an interview. Caesar acceded to the suggestion, and the arrangements for a conference were made, each party, as usual in such cases, taking every precaution to guard against the treachery of the other.

Between the two camps there was a rising ground, in the middle of an open plain, where it was decided that the conference should be held. Ariovistus proposed that neither party should bring any foot soldiers to the place of meeting, but cavalry alone; and that these bodies of cavalry, brought by the respective generals, should remain at the foot of the eminence on either side, while Caesar and Ariovistus themselves, attended each by only ten followers on horseback, should ascend it. This plan was acceded to by Caesar, and a long conference was held in this way between the two generals, as they sat upon their horses, on the summit of the hill.

Conference between Caesar and Ariovistus.

Caesar's messenger seized.

The two generals, in their discussion, only repeated in substance what they had said in their embassages before, and made no progress toward coming to an understanding. At length Caesar closed the conference and withdrew. Some days afterward Ariovistus sent a request to Caesar, asking that he would appoint another interview, or else that he would depute one of his officers to proceed to Ariovistus's camp and receive a communication which he wished to make to him. Caesar concluded not to grant another interview, and he did not think it prudent to send any one of his principal officers as an embassador, for fear that he might be treacherously seized and held as a hostage. He accordingly sent an ordinary messenger, accompanied by one or two men. These men were all seized and put in irons as soon as they reached the camp of Ariovistus, and Caesar now prepared in earnest for giving his enemy battle.

Defeat of the Germans.

He proved himself as skillful and efficient in arranging and managing the combat as he had been sagacious and adroit in the negotiations which preceded it. Several days were spent in maneuvers and movements, by which each party endeavored to gain some advantage over the other in respect to their position in the approaching struggle. When at length the combat came, Caesar and his legions were entirely and triumphantly successful. The Germans were put totally to flight. Their baggage and stores were all seized, and the troops themselves fled in dismay by all the roads which led back to the Rhine; and there those who succeeded in escaping death from the Romans, who pursued them all the way, embarked in boats and upon rafts, and returned to their homes. Ariovistus himself found a small boat, in which, with one or two followers, he succeeded in getting across the stream.

Release of Caesar's messenger.

As Caesar, at the head of a body of his troops, was pursuing the enemy in this their flight, he overtook one party who had a prisoner with them confined by iron chains fastened to his limbs, and whom they were hurrying rapidly along. This prisoner proved to be the messenger that Caesar had sent to Ariovistus's camp, and whom he had, as Caesar alleges, treacherously detained. Of course, he was overjoyed to be recaptured and set at liberty. The man said that three times they had drawn lots to see whether they should burn him alive then, or reserve the pleasure for a future occasion, and that every time the lot had resulted in his favor.

Results of the victory.

Caesar's continued success.

The consequence of this victory was, that Caesar's authority was established triumphantly over all that part of Gaul which he had thus freed from Ariovistus's sway. Other parts of the country, too, were pervaded by the fame of his exploits, and the people every where began to consider what action it would be incumbent on them to take, in respect to the new military power which had appeared so suddenly among them. Some nations determined to submit without resistance, and to seek the conqueror's alliance and protection. Others, more bold, or more confident of their strength, began to form combinations and to arrange plans for resisting him. But, whatever they did, the result in the end was the same. Caesar's ascendency was every where and always gaining ground. Of course, it is impossible in the compass of a single chapter, which is all that can be devoted to the subject in this volume, to give any regular narrative of the events of the eight years of Caesar's military career in Gaul. Marches, negotiations, battles, and victories mingled with and followed each other in a long succession, the particulars of which it would require a volume to detail, every thing resulting most successfully for the increase of Caesar's power and the extension of his fame.

Account of northern nations.

Their strange customs.

Well-trained horses.

Caesar gives, in his narrative, very extraordinary accounts of the customs and modes of life of some of the people that he encountered. There was one country, for example, in which all the lands were common, and the whole structure of society was based on the plan of forming the community into one great martial band. The nation was divided into a hundred cantons, each containing two thousand men capable of bearing arms. If these were all mustered into service together, they would form, of course, an army of two hundred thousand men. It was customary, however, to organize only one half of them into an army, while the rest remained at home to till the ground and tend the flocks and herds. These two great divisions interchanged their work every year, the soldiers becoming husbandmen, and the husbandmen soldiers. Thus they all became equally inured to the hardships and dangers of the camp, and to the more continuous but safer labors of agricultural toil. Their fields were devoted to pasturage more than to tillage, for flocks and herds could be driven from place to place, and thus more easily preserved from the depredations of enemies than fields of grain. The children grew up almost perfectly wild from infancy, and hardened themselves by bathing in cold streams, wearing very little clothing, and making long hunting excursions among the mountains. The people had abundance of excellent horses, which the young men were accustomed, from their earliest years, to ride without saddle or bridle, the horses being trained to obey implicitly every command. So admirably disciplined were they, that sometimes, in battle, the mounted men would leap from their horses and advance as foot soldiers to aid the other infantry, leaving the horses to stand until they returned. The horses would not move from the spot; the men, when the object for which they had dismounted was accomplished, would come back, spring to their seats again, and once more become a squadron of cavalry.

Caesar's popularity with the army.

Caesar's military habits.

His bridge across the Rhine.

Although Caesar was very energetic and decided in the government of his army, he was extremely popular with his soldiers in all these campaigns. He exposed his men, of course, to a great many privations and hardships, but then he evinced, in many cases, such a willingness to bear his share of them, that the men were very little inclined to complain. He moved at the head of the column when his troops were advancing on a march, generally on horseback, but often on foot; and Suetonius says that he used to go bareheaded on such occasions, whatever was the state of the weather, though it is difficult to see what the motive of this apparently needless exposure could be, unless it was for effect, on some special or unusual occasion. Caesar would ford or swim rivers with his men whenever there was no other mode of transit, sometimes supported, it was said, by bags inflated with air, and placed under his arms. At one time he built a bridge across the Rhine, to enable his army to cross that river. This bridge was built with piles driven down into the sand, which supported a flooring of timbers. Caesar, considering it quite an exploit thus to bridge the Rhine, wrote a minute account of the manner in which the work was constructed, and the description is almost exactly in accordance with the principles and usages of modern carpentry.

System of posts.

Their great utility.

After the countries which were the scene of these conquests were pretty well subdued, Caesar established on some of the great routes of travel a system of posts, that is, he stationed supplies of horses at intervals of from ten to twenty miles along the way, so that he himself, or the officers of his army, or any couriers whore he might have occasion to send with dispatches could travel with great speed by finding a fresh horse ready at every stage. By this means he sometimes traveled himself a hundred miles in a day. This system, thus adopted for military purposes in

Caesar's time, has been continued in almost all countries of Europe to the present age, and is applied to traveling in carriages as well as on horseback. A family party purchase a carriage, and arranging within it all the comforts and conveniences which they will require on the journey, they set out, taking these post horses, fresh at each village, to draw them to the next. Thus they can go at any rate of speed which they desire, instead of being limited in their movements by the powers of endurance of one set of animals, as they would be compelled to be if they were to travel with their own. This plan has, for some reason, never been introduced into America, and it is now probable that it never will be, as the railway system will doubtless supersede it.

Caesar's invasion of Britain.

His pretext for it.

One of the most remarkable of the enterprises which Caesar undertook during the period of these campaigns was his excursion into Great Britain. The real motive of this expedition was probably a love of romantic adventure, and a desire to secure for himself at Rome the glory of having penetrated into remote regions which Roman armies had never reached before. The pretext, however, which he made to justify his invading the territories of the Britons was, that the people of the island were accustomed to come across the Channel and aid the Gauls in their wars.

Caesar consults the merchants.

In forming his arrangements for going into England, the first thing was, to obtain all the information which was accessible in Gaul in respect to the country. There were, in those days, great numbers of traveling merchants, who went from one nation to another to purchase and sell, taking with them such goods as were most easy of transportation. These merchants, of course, were generally possessed of a great deal of information in respect to the countries which they had visited, and Caesar called together as many of them as he could find, when he had reached the northern shores of France, to inquire about the modes of crossing the Channel, the harbors on the English side, the geographical conformation of the country, and the military resources of the people. He found, however, that the merchants could give him very little information. They knew that Britain was an island, but they did not know its extent or its boundaries; and they could tell him very little of the character or customs of the people. They said that they had only been accustomed to land upon the southern shore, and to transact all their business there, without penetrating at all into the interior of the country.

Volusenus.

Caesar then, who, though undaunted and bold in emergencies requiring prompt and decisive action, was extremely cautious and wary at all other times, fitted up a single ship, and, putting one of his officers on board with a proper crew, directed him to cross the Channel to the English coast, and then to cruise along the land for some miles in each direction, to observe where were the best harbors and places for landing, and to examine generally the appearance of the shore. This vessel was a galley, manned with numerous oarsmen, well selected and strong, so that it could retreat with great speed from any sudden appearance of danger The name of the officer who had the command of it was Volusenus. Volusenus set sail, the army watching his vessel with great interest as it moved slowly away from the shore. He was gone five days, and then returned, bringing Caesar an account of his discoveries.

Caesar collects vessels.

In the mean time, Caesar had collected a large number of sailing vessels from the whole line of the French shore, by means of which he proposed to transport his army across the Channel. He had two legions to take into Britain, the remainder of his forces having been stationed as garrisons in various parts of Gaul. It was necessary, too, to leave a considerable force at his post of debarkation, in order to secure a safe retreat in case of any disaster on the British side. The number of transport ships provided for the foot soldiers which were to be taken over was eighty. There were, besides these, eighteen more, which were appointed to convey a squadron of horse. This cavalry force was to embark at a separate port, about eighty miles distant from the one from which the infantry were to sail.

Embarkation of the troops.

At length a suitable day for the embarkation arrived; the troops were put on board the ships, and orders were given to sail. The day could not be fixed beforehand, as the time for attempting to make the passage must necessarily depend upon the state of the wind and weather. Accordingly, when the favorable opportunity arrived, and the main body of the army began to embark it took some time to send the orders to the port where the cavalry had rendezvoused; and there were, besides, other causes of delay which occurred to detain this corps, so that it turned out, as we shall presently see, that the foot soldiers had to act alone in the first attempt at landing on the British shore.

Sailing of the fleet.

Preparations of the Britons.

It was one o'clock in the morning when the fleet set sail. The Britons had, in the mean time, obtained intelligence of Caesar's threatened invasion, and they had assembled in great force, with troops, and horsemen, and carriages of war, and were all ready to guard the shore. The coast, at the point where Caesar was approaching, consists of a line of chalky cliffs, with valley-like openings here and there between them, communicating with the shore, and sometimes narrow beaches below. When the Roman fleet approached the land, Caesar found the cliffs every where lined with troops of Britons, and every accessible point below carefully guarded. It was now about ten o'clock in the morning, and Caesar, finding the prospect so unfavorable in respect to the practicability of effecting a landing here, brought his fleet to anchor near the shore, but far enough from it to be safe from the missiles of the enemy.

Caesar calls a council of officers.

Here he remained for several hours, to give time for all the vessels to join him. Some of them had been delayed in the embarkation, or had made slower progress than the rest in crossing the Channel. He called a council, too, of the superior officers of the army on board his own galley, and explained to them the plan which he now adopted for the landing. About three o'clock in the afternoon he sent these officers back to their respective ships, and gave orders to make sail along the shore. The anchors were raised and the fleet moved on, borne by the united impulse of the wind and the tide. The Britons, perceiving this movement, put themselves in motion on the land, following the motions of the fleet so as to be ready to meet their enemy wherever they might ultimately undertake to land. Their horsemen and carriages went on in advance, and the foot soldiers followed, all pressing eagerly forward to keep up with the motion of the fleet, and to prevent Caesar's army from having time to land before they should arrive at the spot and be ready to oppose them.

THE LANDING IN ENGLAND.

The landing.

The battle.

Defeat of the Britons.

The fleet moved on until, at length, after sailing about eight miles, they came to a part of the coast where there was a tract of comparatively level ground, which seemed to be easily accessible from the shore. Here Caesar determined to attempt to land; and drawing up his vessel, accordingly, as near as possible to the beach, he ordered the men to leap over into the water, with their weapons in their hands. The Britons were all here to oppose them, and a dreadful struggle ensued, the combatants dyeing the waters with their blood as they fought, half submerged in the surf which rolled in upon the sand. Some galleys rowed up at the same time near to the shore, and the men on board of them attacked the Britons from the decks, by the darts and arrows which they shot to the land. Caesar at last prevailed; the Britons were driven away, and the Roman army established themselves in quiet possession of the shore.

Caesar's popularity at Rome.

Caesar had afterward a great variety of adventures, and many narrow escapes from imminent dangers in Britain, and, though he gained considerable glory by thus penetrating into such remote and unknown regions, there was very little else to be acquired. The glory, however, was itself of great value to Caesar. During the whole period of his campaigns in Gaul, Rome and all Italy in fact, had been filled with the fame of his exploits, and the expedition into Britain added not a little to his renown. The populace of the city were greatly gratified to hear of the continued success of their former favorite. They decreed to him triumph after triumph, and were prepared to welcome him, whenever he should return, with greater honors and more extended and higher powers than he had ever enjoyed before.

Results of his campaigns.

Caesar's exploits in these campaigns were, in fact, in a military point of view, of the most magnificent character. Plutarch, in summing up the results of them, says that he took eight hundred cities, conquered three hundred nations, fought pitched battles at separate times with three millions of men, took one million of prisoners, and killed another million on the field. What a vast work of destruction was this for a man to spend eight years of his life in performing upon his fellow-creatures, merely to gratify his insane love of dominion.

### CHAPTER V.: POMPEY.

Pompey.

While Caesar had thus been rising to so high an elevation, there was another Roman general who had been, for nearly the same period, engaged, in various other quarters of the world, in acquiring, by very similar means, an almost equal renown. This general was Pompey. He became, in the end, Caesar's great and formidable rival. In order that the reader may understand clearly the nature of the great contest which sprung up at last between these heroes, we must now go back and relate some of the particulars of Pompey's individual history down to the time of the completion of Caesar's conquests in Gaul.

His birth.

Pompey's personal appearance.

Pompey was a few years older than Caesar, having been born in 106 B.C. His father was a Roman general, and the young Pompey was brought up in camp. He was a young man of very handsome figure and countenance, and of very agreeable manners. His hair curled slightly over his forehead, and he had a dark and intelligent eye, full of vivacity and meaning. There was, besides, in the expression of his face, and in his air and address, a certain indescribable charm, which prepossessed every one strongly in his favor, and gave him, from his earliest years, a great personal ascendency over all who knew him.

Plans to assassinate him.

Notwithstanding this popularity, however, Pompey did not escape, even in very early life, incurring his share of the dangers which seemed to environ the path of every public man in those distracted times. It will be recollected that, in the contests between Marius and Sylla, Caesar had joined the Marian faction. Pompey's father, on the other hand, had connected himself with that of Sylla. At one time, in the midst of these wars, when Pompey was very young, a conspiracy was formed to assassinate his father by burning him in his tent, and Pompey's comrade, named Terentius, who slept in the same tent with him, had been bribed to kill Pompey himself at the same time, by stabbing him in his bed. Pompey contrived to discover this plan, but, instead of being at all discomposed by it, he made arrangements for a guard about his father's tent and then went to supper as usual with Terentius, conversing with him all the time in even a more free and friendly manner than usual. That night he arranged his bed so as to make it appear as if he was in it, and then stole away. When the appointed hour arrived, Terentius came into the tent, and, approaching the couch where he supposed Pompey was lying asleep, stabbed it again and again, piercing the coverlets in many places, but doing no harm, of course, to his intended victim.

Pompey's adventures and escapes.

Death of his father.

Pompey appears in his father's defense.

In the course of the wars between Marius and Sylla, Pompey passed through a great variety of scenes, and met with many extraordinary adventures and narrow escapes, which, however, can not be here particularly detailed. His father, who was as much hated by his soldiers as the son was beloved, was at last, one day, struck by lightning in his tent. The soldiers were inspired with such a hatred for his memory, in consequence, probably, of the cruelties and oppressions which they had suffered from him, that they would not allow his body to be honored with the ordinary funeral obsequies. They pulled it off from the bier on which it was to have been borne to the funeral pile, and dragged it ignominiously away. Pompey's father was accused, too, after his death, of having converted some public moneys which had been committed to his charge to his own use, and Pompey appeared in the Roman Forum as an advocate to defend him from the charge and to vindicate his memory. He was very successful in this defense. All who heard it were, in the first instance, very deeply interested in favor of the speaker, on account of his extreme youth and his personal beauty; and, as he proceeded with his plea, he argued with so much eloquence and power as to win universal applause. One of the chief officers of the government in the city was so much pleased with his appearance, and with the promise of future greatness which the circumstances indicated, that he offered him his daughter in marriage. Pompey accepted the offer, and married the lady. Her name was Antistia.

His success as a general.

Pompey defeats the armies.

Pompey rose rapidly to higher and higher degrees of distinction, until he obtained the command of an army, which he had, in fact, in a great measure raised and organized himself, and he fought at the head of it with great energy and success against the enemies of Sylla. At length he was hemmed in on the eastern coast of Italy by three separate armies, which were gradually advancing against him, with a certainty, as they thought, of effecting his destruction. Sylla, hearing of Pompey's danger, made great efforts to march to his rescue. Before he reached the place, however, Pompey had met and defeated one after another of the armies of his enemies, so that, when Sylla approached, Pompey marched out to meet him with his army drawn up in magnificent array, trumpets sounding and banners flying, and with large bodies of disarmed troops, the prisoners that he had taken, in the rear. Sylla was struck with surprise and admiration; and when Pompey saluted him with the title of Imperator, which was the highest title known to the Roman constitution, and the one which Sylla's lofty rank and unbounded power might properly claim, Sylla returned the compliment by conferring this great mark of distinction on him.

His rising fame.

Pompey's modesty.

Pompey proceeded to Rome, and the fame of his exploits, the singular fascination of his person and manners, and the great favor with Sylla that he enjoyed, raised him to a high degree of distinction. He was not, however, elated with the pride and vanity which so young a man would be naturally expected to exhibit under such circumstances. He was, on the contrary, modest and unassuming, and he acted in all respects in such a manner as to gain the approbation and the kind regard of all who knew him, as well as to excite their applause. There was an old general at this time in Gaul--for all these events took place long before the time of Caesar's campaigns in that country, and, in fact, before the commencement of his successful career in Rome--whose name was Metellus, and who, either on account of his advancing age, or for some other reason, was very inefficient and unsuccessful in his government. Sylla proposed to supersede him by sending Pompey to take his place. Pompey replied that it was not right to take the command from a man who was so much his superior in age and character, but that, if Metellus wished for his assistance in the management of his command, he would proceed to Gaul and render him every service in his power. When this answer was reported to Metellus, he wrote to Pompey to come. Pompey accordingly went to Gaul, where he obtained new victories, and gained new and higher honors than before.

An example.

Pompey divorces his wife.

He marries Sylla's daughter-in-law.

These, and various anecdotes which the ancient historians relate, would lead us to form very favorable ideas of Pompey's character. Some other circumstances, however, which occurred, seem to furnish different indications. For example, on his return to Rome, some time after the events above related, Sylla, whose estimation of Pompey's character and of the importance of his services seemed continually to increase, wished to connect him with his own family by marriage. He accordingly proposed that Pompey should divorce his wife Antistia, and marry Aemilia, the daughter-in-law of Sylla. Aemilia was already the wife of another man, from whom she would have to be taken away to make her the wife of Pompey. This, however, does not seem to have been thought a very serious difficulty in the way of the arrangement. Pompey's wife was put away, and the wife of another man taken in her place. Such a deed was a gross violation not merely of revealed and written law, but of those universal instincts of right and wrong which are implanted indelibly in all human hearts. It ended, as might have been expected, most disastrously. Antistia was plunged, of course, into the deepest distress. Her father had recently lost his life on account of his supposed attachment to Pompey. Her mother killed herself in the anguish and despair produced by the misfortunes of her family; and Aemilia the new wife, died suddenly, on the occasion of the birth of a child, a very short time after her marriage with Pompey.

Pompey's success in Africa.

Attachment of his soldiers.

Pompey's title as "Great."

These domestic troubles did not, however, interpose any serious obstacle to Pompey's progress in his career of greatness and glory. Sylla sent him on one great enterprise after another, in all of which Pompey acquitted himself in an admirable manner. Among his other campaigns, he served for some time in Africa with great success. He returned in due time from this expedition, loaded with military honors. His soldiers had become so much attached to him that there was almost a mutiny in the army when he was ordered home. They were determined to submit to no authority but that of Pompey. Pompey at length succeeded, by great efforts, in subduing this spirit, and bringing back the army to their duty. A false account of the affair, however, went to Rome. It was reported to Sylla that there was a revolt in the army of Africa, headed by Pompey himself, who was determined not to resign his command. Sylla was at first very indignant that his authority should be despised and his power braved, as he expressed it, by "such a boy;" for Pompey was still, at this time, very young. When, however, he learned the truth, he conceived a higher admiration for the young general than ever. He went out to meet him as he approached the city, and, in accosting him, he called him Pompey the Great. Pompey has continued to bear the title thus given him to the present day.

He demands a triumph.

Pompey began, it seems, now to experience, in some degree, the usual effects produced upon the human heart by celebrity and praise. He demanded a triumph. A triumph was a great and splendid ceremony, by which victorious generals, who were of advanced age and high civil or military rank, were received into the city when returning from any specially glorious campaign. There was a grand procession formed on these occasions, in which various emblems and insignia, and trophies of victory, and captives taken by the conqueror, were displayed. This great procession entered the city with bands of music accompanying it, and flags and banners flying, passing under triumphal arches erected along the way. Triumphs were usually decreed by a vote of the Senate, in cases where they were deserved; but, in this case, Sylla's power as dictator was supreme, and Pompey's demand for a triumph seems to have been addressed accordingly to him.

Sylla refuses Pompey a triumph.

Sylla refused it. Pompey's performances in the African campaign had been, he admitted, very creditable to him, but he had neither the Age nor the rank to justify the granting him a triumph. To bestow such an honor upon one so young and in such a station, would only bring the honor itself, he said, into disrepute, and degrade, also, his dictatorship for suffering it.

But at last consents.

To this Pompey replied, speaking, however, in an under tone to those around him in the assembly, that Sylla need not fear that the triumph would be unpopular, for people were much more disposed to worship a rising than a setting sun. Sylla did not hear this remark, but, perceiving by the countenances of the by-standers that Pompey had said something which seemed to please them, he asked what it was. When the remark was repeated to him, he seemed pleased himself with its justness or with its wit, and said, "Let him have his triumph."

Pompey's triumph.

The arrangements were accordingly made Pompey ordering every thing necessary to be prepared for a most magnificent procession. He learned that some persons in the city, envious at his early renown, were displeased with his triumph; this only awakened in him a determination to make it still more splendid and imposing. He had brought some elephants with him from Africa, and he formed a plan for having the car in which he was to ride in the procession drawn by four of these huge beasts as it entered the city; but, on measuring the gate, it was found not wide enough to admit such a team, and the plan was accordingly abandoned. The conqueror's car was drawn by horses in the usual manner, and the elephants followed singly, with the other trophies, to grace the train.

His course of conduct at Rome.

Pompey remained some time after this in Rome, sustaining from time to time various offices of dignity and honor. His services were often called for to plead causes in the Forum, and he performed this duty, whenever he undertook it, with great success. He, however, seemed generally inclined to retire somewhat from intimate intercourse with the mass of the community, knowing very well that if he was engaged often in the discussion of common questions with ordinary men, he should soon descend in public estimation from the high position to which his military renown had raised him. He accordingly accustomed himself to appear but little in public, and, when he did so appear, he was generally accompanied by a large retinue of armed attendants, at the head of which he moved about the city in great state, more like a victorious general in a conquered province than like a peaceful citizen exercising ordinary official functions in a community governed by law. This was a very sagacious course, so far as concerned the attainment of the great objects of future ambition. Pompey knew very well that occasions would probably arise in which he could act far more effectually for the promotion of his own greatness and fame than by mingling in the ordinary municipal contests of the city.

The Cilician pirates.

Their increasing depredations.

Ships and fortresses of the Cilicians.

Their conquests.

At length, in fact, an occasion came. In the year B.C. 67, which was about the time that Caesar commenced his successful career in rising to public office in Rome, as is described in the third chapter of this volume, the Cilician pirates, of whose desperate character and bold exploits something has already been said, had become so powerful, and were increasing so rapidly in the extent of their depredations, that the Roman people felt compelled to adopt some very vigorous measures for suppressing them. The pirates had increased in numbers during the wars between Marius and Sylla in a very alarming degree. They had built, equipped, and organized whole fleets. They had various fortresses, arsenals, ports, and watch-towers all along the coasts of the Mediterranean. They had also extensive warehouses, built in secure and secluded places, where they stored their plunder. Their fleets were well manned, and provided with skillful pilots, and with ample supplies of every kind; and they were so well constructed, both for speed and safety, that no other ships could be made to surpass them. Many of them, too, were adorned and decorated in the most sumptuous manner, with gilded sterns, purple awnings, and silver-mounted oars. The number of their galleys was said to be a thousand. With this force they made themselves almost complete masters of the sea. They attacked not only separate ships, but whole fleets of merchantmen sailing under convoy; and they increased the difficulty and expense of bringing grain to Rome so much, by intercepting the supplies, as very materially to enhance the price and to threaten a scarcity. They made themselves masters of many islands and of various maritime towns along the coast, until they had four hundred ports and cities in their possession. In fact, they had gone so far toward forming themselves into a regular maritime power, under a systematic and legitimate government, that very respectable young men from other countries began to enter their service, as one opening honorable avenues to wealth and fame.

Plan for destroying the pirates.

Its magnitude.

Under these circumstances, it was obvious that something decisive must be done. A friend of Pompey's brought forward a plan for commissioning some one, he did not say whom, but every one understood that Pompey was intended, to be sent forth against the pirates, with extraordinary powers, such as should be amply sufficient to enable him to bring their dominion to an end. He was to have supreme command upon the sea, and also upon the land for fifty miles from the shore. He was, moreover, to be empowered to raise as large a force, both of ships and men, as he should think required, and to draw from the treasury whatever funds were necessary to defray the enormous expenses which so vast an undertaking would involve. If the law should pass creating this office, and a person be designated to fill it, it is plain that such a commander would be clothed with enormous powers; but then he would incur, on the other hand, a vast and commensurate responsibility, as the Roman people would hold him rigidly accountable for the full and perfect accomplishment of the work he under took, after they had thus surrendered every possible power necessary to accomplish it so unconditionally into his hands.

Pompey appointed to the command.

Fall in the price of grain.

/p>

There was a great deal of maneuvering, management, and debate on the one hand to effect the passage of this law, and, on the other, to defeat it. Caesar, who, though not so prominent yet as Pompey, was now rising rapidly to influence and power, was in favor of the measure, because, as is said, he perceived that the people were pleased with it. It was at length adopted. Pompey was then designated to fill the office which the law created. He accepted the trust, and began to prepare for the vast undertaking. The price of grain fell immediately in Rome, as soon as the appointment of Pompey was made known, as the merchants, who had large supplies in the granaries there, were now eager to sell, even at a reduction, feeling confident that Pompey's measures would result in bringing in abundant supplies. The people, surprised at this sudden relaxation of the pressure of their burdens, said that the very name of Pompey had put an end to the war.

Pompey's complete success.

They were not mistaken in their anticipations of Pompey's success. He freed the Mediterranean from pirates in three months, by one systematic and simple operation, which affords one of the most striking examples of the power of united and organized effort, planned and conducted by one single master mind, which the history of ancient or modern times has recorded. The manner in which this work was effected was this:

His mode of operation.

Pompey raised and equipped a vast number of galleys, and divided them into separate fleets, putting each one under the command of a lieutenant. He then divided the Mediterranean Sea into thirteen districts, and appointed a lieutenant and his fleet for each one of them as a guard. After sending these detachments forth to their respective stations, he set out from the city himself to take charge of the operations which he was to conduct in person. The people followed him, as he went to the place where he was to embark, in great crowds, and with long and loud acclamations.

Pompey drives the pirates before him.

Exultation at Rome.

Beginning at the Straits of Gibraltar, Pompey cruised with a powerful fleet toward the east, driving the pirates before him, the lieutenants, who were stationed along the coast being on the alert to prevent them from finding any places of retreat or refuge. Some of the pirates' ships were surrounded and taken. Others fled, and were followed by Pompey's ships until they had passed beyond the coasts of Sicily, and the seas between the Italian and African shores. The communication was now open again to the grain-growing countries south of Rome, and large supplies of food were immediately poured into the city. The whole population was, of course, filled with exultation and joy at receiving such welcome proofs that Pompey was successfully accomplishing the work they had assigned him.

The pirates concentrate themselves.

The Italian peninsula and the island of Sicily, which are, in fact, a projection from the northern shores of the Mediterranean, with a salient angle of the coast nearly opposite to them on the African side, form a sort of strait which divides this great sea into two separate bodies of water, and the pirates were now driven entirely out of the western division. Pompey sent his principal fleet after them, with orders to pass around the island of Sicily and the south era part of Italy to Brundusium, which was the great port on the western side of Italy. He himself was to cross the peninsula by land, taking Rome in his way, and afterward to join the fleet at Brundusium. The pirates, in the mean time, so far as they had escaped Pompey's cruisers, had retreated to the seas in the neighborhood of Cilicia, and were concentrating their forces there in preparation for the final struggle.

Pompey was received at Rome with the utmost enthusiasm. The people came out in throngs to meet him as he approached the city, and welcomed him with loud acclamations. He did not, however, remain in the city to enjoy these honors. He procured, as soon as possible, what was necessary for the further prosecution of his work, and went on. He found his fleet at Brundusium, and, immediately embarking, he put to sea.

Some of them surrender.

Pompey went on to the completion of his work with the same vigor and decision which he had displayed in the commencement of it. Some of the pirates, finding themselves hemmed in within narrower and narrower limits, gave up the contest, and came and surrendered. Pompey, instead of punishing them severely for their crimes, treated them, and their wives and children, who fell likewise into his power, with great humanity. This induced many others to follow their example, so that the number that remained resisting to the end was greatly reduced. There were, however, after all these submissions, a body of stern and indomitable desperadoes left, who were incapable of yielding. These retreated, with all the forces which they could retain, to their strong-holds on the Silician shores, sending their wives and children back to still securer retreats among the fastnesses of the mountains.

A great battle.

Disposal of the pirates.

Pompey followed them, hemming them in with the squadrons of armed galleys which he brought up around them, thus cutting off from them all possibility of escape. Here, at length, a great final battle was fought, and the dominion of the pirates was ended forever. Pompey destroyed their ships, dismantled their fortifications, restored the harbors and towns which they had seized to their rightful owners, and sent the pirates themselves, with their wives and children, far into the interior of the country, and established them as agriculturists and herdsmen there, in a territory which he set apart for the purpose, where they might live in peace on the fruits of their own industry, without the possibility of again disturbing the commerce of the seas.

Pompey's conquests in Asia Minor.

His magnificent triumph.

Instead of returning to Rome after these exploits, Pompey obtained new powers from the government of the city, and pushed his way into Asia Minor, where he remained several years, pursuing a similar career of conquest to that of Caesar in Gaul. At length he returned to Rome, his entrance into the city being signalized by a most magnificent triumph. The procession for displaying the trophies, the captives, and the other emblems of victory, and for conveying the vast accumulation of treasures and spoils, was two days in passing into the city; and enough was left after all for another triumph. Pompey was, in a word, on the very summit of human grandeur and renown.

The first triumvirate.

Pompey's wife Julia.

Pompey and Caesar open enemies.

Their ambition.

He found, however, an old enemy and rival at Rome. This was Crassus, who had been Pompey's opponent in earlier times, and who now renewed his hostility. In the contest that ensued, Pompey relied on his renown, Crassus on his wealth. Pompey attempted to please the people by combats of lions and of elephants which he had brought home from his foreign campaigns; Crassus courted their favor by distributing corn among them, and inviting them to public feasts on great occasions. He spread for them, at one time, it was said, ten thousand tables. All Rome was filled with the feuds of these great political foes. It was at this time that Caesar returned from Spain, and had the adroitness, as has already been explained, to extinguish these feuds, and reconcile these apparently implacable foes. He united them together, and joined them with himself in a triple league, which is celebrated in Roman history as the first triumvirate. The rivalry, however, of these great aspirants for power was only suppressed and concealed, without being at all weakened or changed. The death of Crassus soon removed him from the stage. Caesar and Pompey continued afterward, for some time, an ostensible alliance. Caesar attempted to strengthen this bond by giving Pompey his daughter Julia for his wife. Julia, though so young--even her father was six years younger than Pompey--was devotedly attached to her husband, and he was equally fond of her. She formed, in fact, a strong bond of union between the two great conquerors as long as she lived. One day, however, there was a riot at an election, and men were killed so near to Pompey that his robe was covered with blood. He changed it; the servants carried home the bloody garment which he had taken off, and Julia was so terrified at the sight, thinking that her husband had been killed, that she fainted, and her constitution suffered very severely by the shock. She lived some time afterward, but finally died under circumstances which indicate that this occurrence was the cause. Pompey and Caesar now soon became open enemies. The ambitious aspirations which each of them cherished were so vast, that the world was not wide enough for them both to be satisfied. They had assisted each other up the ascent which they had been so many years in climbing, but now they had reached very near to the summit, and the question was to be decided which of the two should have his station there.

## CHAPTER VI.: CROSSING THE RUBICON.

The Rubicon.

There was a little stream in ancient times, in the north of Italy, which flowed westward into the Adriatic Sea, called the Rubicon. This stream has been immortalized by the transactions which we are now about to describe.

Its insignificance as a stream.

The Rubicon was a very important boundary, and yet it was in itself so small and insignificant that it is now impossible to determine which of two or three little brooks here running into the sea is entitled to its name and renown. In history the Rubicon is a grand, permanent, and conspicuous stream, gazed upon with continued interest by all mankind for nearly twenty centuries; in nature it is an uncertain rivulet, for a long time doubtful and undetermined, and finally lost.

Importance of the Rubicon as a boundary.

The Rubicon originally derived its importance from the fact that it was the boundary between all that part of the north of Italy which is formed by the valley of the Po, one of the richest and most magnificent countries of the world, and the more southern Roman territories. This country of the Po constituted what was in those days called the hither Gaul, and was a Roman province. It belonged now to Caesar's jurisdiction, as the commander in Gaul. All south of the Rubicon was territory reserved for the immediate jurisdiction of the city. The Romans, in order to protect themselves from any danger which might threaten their own liberties from the immense armies which they raised for the conquest of foreign nations, had imposed on every side very strict limitations and restrictions in respect to the approach of these armies to the Capitol. The Rubicon was the limit on this northern side. Generals commanding in Gaul were never to pass it. To cross the Rubicon with an army on the way to Rome was rebellion and treason. Hence the Rubicon became, as it were, the visible sign and symbol of civil restriction to military power.

Caesar's expenditure of money at Rome.

His influence.

As Caesar found the time of his service in Gaul drawing toward a conclusion, he turned his thoughts more and more toward Rome, endeavoring to strengthen his interest there by every means in his power, and to circumvent and thwart the designs of Pompey. He had and partisans in Rome who acted for him and in his name. He sent immense sums of money to these men, to be employed in such ways as would most tend to secure the favor of the people. He ordered the Forum to be rebuilt with great magnificence. He arranged great celebrations, in which the people were entertained with an endless succession of games, spectacles, and public feasts. When his daughter Julia, Pompey's wife, died, he celebrated her funeral with indescribable splendor. He distributed corn in immense quantities among the people, and he sent a great many captives home, to be trained as gladiators, to fight in the theaters for their amusement. In many cases, too, where he found men of talents and influence among the populace, who had become involved in debt by their dissipations and extravagance, he paid their debts, and thus secured their influence on his side. Men were astounded at the magnitude of these expenditures, and, while the multitude rejoiced thoughtlessly in the pleasures thus provided for them, the more reflecting and considerate trembled at the greatness of the power which was so rapidly rising to overshadow the land.

Pompey's personal popularity.

Public thanksgiving in his behalf.

It increased their anxiety to observe that Pompey was gaining the same kind of influence and ascendency too. He had not the advantage which Caesar enjoyed in the prodigious wealth obtained from the rich countries over which Caesar ruled, but he possessed, instead of it, the advantage of being all the time at Rome, and of securing, by his character and action there, a very wide personal popularity and influence. Pompey was, in fact, the idol of the people. At one time, when he was absent from Rome, at Naples, he was taken sick. After being for some days in considerable danger, the crisis passed favorably, and he recovered. Some of the people of Naples proposed a public thanksgiving to the gods, to celebrate his restoration to health. The plan was adopted by acclamation, and the example, thus set, extended from city to city, until it had spread throughout Italy, and the whole country was filled with the processions, games, shows, and celebrations, which were instituted every where in honor of the event. And when Pompey returned from Naples to Rome, the towns on the way could not afford room for the crowds that came forth to meet him. The high roads, the villages, the ports, says Plutarch, were filled with sacrifices and entertainments. Many received him with garlands on their heads and torches in their hands, and, as they conducted him along, strewed the way with flowers.

Pompey's estimate of Caesar's power.

In fact, Pompey considered himself as standing far above Caesar in fame and power, and this general burst of enthusiasm and applause, educed by his recovery from sickness, confirmed him in this idea. He felt no solicitude, he said, in respect to Caesar. He should take no special precautions against any hostile designs which he might entertain on his return from Gaul. It was he himself, he said, that had raised Caesar up to whatever of elevation he had attained, and he could put him down even more easily than he had exalted him.

Plans of the latter.

In the mean time, the period was drawing near in which Caesar's command in the provinces was to expire; and, anticipating the struggle with Pompey which was about to ensue, he conducted several of his legions through the passes of the Alps, and advanced gradually, as he had a right to do, across the country of the Po toward the Rubicon, revolving in his capacious mind, as he came, the various plans by which he might hope to gain the ascendency over the power of his mighty rival, and make himself supreme.

Caesar arrives at Ravenna.

Pompey's demands.

He concluded that it would be his wisest policy not to a'tempt to intimidate Pompey by great and open preparations for war, which might tend to arouse him to vigorous measures of resistance, but rather to cover and conceal his designs, and thus throw his enemy off his guard.

He advanced, therefore, toward the Rubicon with a small force. He established his headquarters at Ravenna, a city not far from the river, and employed himself in objects of local interest there, in order to avert as much as possible the minds of the people from imagining that he was contemplating any great design. Pompey sent to him to demand the return of a certain legion which he had lent him from his own army at a time when they were friends. Caesar complied with this demand without any hesitation, and sent the legion home. He sent with this legion, also, some other troops which were properly his own, thus evincing a degree of indifference in respect to the amount of the force retained under his command which seemed wholly inconsistent with the idea that he contemplated any resistance to the authority of the government at Rome.

Caesar demands to be made consul.

Excitement in consequence.

In the mean time, the struggle at Rome between the partisans of Caesar and Pompey grew more and more violent and alarming. Caesar through his friends in the city, demanded to be elected consul. The other side insisted that he must first, if that was his wish, resign the command of his army, come to Rome, and present himself as a candidate in the character of a private citizen. This the constitution of the state very properly required. In answer to this requisition, Caesar rejoined, that, if Pompey would lay down his military commands, he would do so too; if not, it was unjust to require it of him. The services, he added, which he had performed for his country, demanded some recompense, which, moreover, they ought to be willing to award, even if, in order to do it, it were necessary to relax somewhat in his favor the strictness of ordinary rules. To a large part of the people of the city these demands of Caesar appeared reasonable. They were clamorous to have them allowed. The partisans of Pompey, with the stern and inflexible Cato at their head, deemed them wholly inadmissible, and contended with the most determined violence against them. The whole city was filled with the excitement of this struggle, into which all the active and turbulent spirits of the capital plunged with the most furious zeal, while the more considerate and thoughtful of the population, remembering the days of Marius and Sylla, trembled at the impending danger. Pompey himself had no fear. He urged the Senate to resist to the utmost all of Caesar's claims, saying, if Caesar should be so presumptuous as to attempt to march to Rome, he could raise troops enough by stamping with his foot to put him down.

Debates in the Senate.

Tumult and confusion.

Panic at Rome.

It would require a volume to contain a full account of the disputes and tumults, the maneuvers and debates, the votes and decrees which marked the successive stages of this quarrel. Pompey himself was all the time without the city. He was in command of an army there, and no general, while in command, was allowed to come within the gates. At last an exciting debate was broken up in the Senate by one of the consuls rising to depart, saying that he would hear the subject discussed no longer. The time had arrived for action, and he should send a commander, with an armed force, to defend the country from Caesar's threatened invasion. Caesar's leading friends, two tribunes of the people, disguised themselves as slaves, and fled to the north to join their master. The country was filled with commotion and panic. The Commonwealth had obviously more fear of Caesar than confidence in Pompey. The country was full of rumors in respect to Caesar's power, and the threatening attitude which he was assuming, while they who had insisted on resistance seemed, after all, to have provided very inadequate means with which to resist. A thousand plans were formed, and clamorously insisted upon by their respective advocates, for averting the danger. This only added to the confusion, and the city became at length pervaded with a universal terror.

Caesar at Ravenna.

While this was the state of things at Rome, Caesar was quietly established at Ravenna; thirty or forty miles from the frontier. He was erecting a building for a fencing school there and his mind seemed to be occupied very busily with the plans and models of the edifice which the architects had formed. Of course, in his intended march to Rome, his reliance was not to be so much on the force which he should take with him, as on the co-operation and support which he expected to find there. It was his policy, therefore, to move as quietly and privately as possible, and with as little display of violence, and to avoid every thing which might indicate his intended march to any spies which might be around him, or to any other person! who might be disposed to report what they observed at Rome. Accordingly, on the very eve of his departure, he busied himself with his fencing school, and assumed with his officers and soldiers a careless and unconcerned air, which prevented any one from suspecting his design.

Caesar's midnight march.

He loses his way.

In the course of the day he privately sent forward some cohorts to the southward, with orders for them to encamp on the banks of the Rubicon. When night came he sat down to supper as usual, and conversed with his friends in his ordinary manner, and went with them afterward to a public entertainment. As soon as it was dark and the streets were still, he set off secretly from the city, accompanied by a very few attendants. Instead of making use of his ordinary equipage, the parading of which would have attracted attention to his movements, he had some mules taken from a neighboring bake-house, and harnessed into his chaise. There were torch-bearers provided to light the way. The cavalcade drove on during the night, finding, however, the hasty preparations which had been made inadequate for the occasion. The torches went out, the guides lost their way, and the future conqueror of the world wandered about bewildered and lost, until, just after break of day, the party met with a peasant who undertook to guide them. Under his direction they made their way to the main road again, and advanced then without further difficulty to the banks of the river, where they found that portion of the army which had been sent forward encamped, and awaiting their arrival.

CROSSING THE RUBICON.

Caesar at the Rubicon.

His hesitation at the river.

Caesar stood for some time upon the banks of the stream, musing upon the greatness of the undertaking in which simply passing across it would involve him. His officers stood by his side.

"We can retreat now" said he, "but once across that river and we must go on." He paused for some time, conscious of the vast importance of the decision, though he thought only, doubtless, of its consequences to himself. Taking the step which was now before him would necessarily end either in his realizing the loftiest aspirations of his ambition, or in his utter and irreparable ruin. There were vast public interests, too, at stake, of which, however he probably thought but little. It proved, in the end, that the history of the whole Roman world, for several centuries, was depending upon the manner in which the question new in Caesar's mind should turn.

Story of the shepherd trumpeter.

There was a little bridge across the Rubicon at the point where Caesar was surveying it. While he was standing there, the story is, a peasant or shepherd came from the neighboring fields with a shepherd's pipe--a simple musical instrument, made of a reed, and used much by the rustic musicians of those days. The soldiers and some of the officers gathered around him to hear him play. Among the rest came some of Caesar's trumpeters, with their trumpets in their hands. The shepherd took one of these martial instruments from the hands of its possessor, laying aside his own, and began to sound a charge--which is a signal for a rapid advance--and to march at the same time over the bridge "An omen! a prodigy!" said Caesar. "Let us march where we are called by such a divine intimation. The die is cast."

Caesar crosses the Rubicon.

So saying, he pressed forward over the bridge, while the officers, breaking up the encampment, put the columns in motion to follow him.

It was shown abundantly, on many occasions in the course of Caesar's life, that he had no faith in omens. There are equally numerous instances to show that he was always ready to avail himself of the popular belief in them; to awaken his soldiers' ardor or to allay their fears. Whether, therefore, in respect to this story of the shepherd trumpeter, it was an incident that really and accidentally occurred, or whether Caesar planned and arranged it himself, with reference to its effect, or whether, which is, perhaps, after all, the most probable supposition, the tale was only an embellishment invented out of something or nothing by the story-tellers of those days, to give additional dramatic interest to the narrative of the crossing of the Rubicon, it must be left for each reader to decide.

Caesar assembles his troops.

His address to them.

As soon as the bridge was crossed, Caesar called an assembly of his troops, and, with signs of great excitement and agitation, made an address to them on the magnitude of the crisis through which they were passing. He showed them how entirely he was in their power; he urged them, by the most eloquent appeals, to stand by him, faithful and true, promising them the most ample rewards when he should have attained the object at which he aimed. The soldiers responded to this appeal with promises of the most unwavering fidelity.

Surrender of various towns.

The first town on the Roman side of the Rubicon was Ariminum. Caesar advanced to this town. The authorities opened its gates to him--very willing, as it appeared, to receive him as their commander. Caesar's force was yet quite small, as he had been accompanied by only a single legion in crossing the river. He had, however, sent orders for the other legions, which had been left in Gaul, to join him without any delay, though any re-enforcement of his troops seemed hardly necessary, as he found no indications of opposition to his progress. He gave his soldiers the strictest injunctions to do no injury to any property, public or private, as they advanced, and not to assume, in any respect, a hostile attitude toward the people of the country. The inhabitants, therefore, welcomed him wherever he came, and all the cities and towns followed the example of Ariminum, surrendering, in fact, faster than he could take possession of them.

Domitius appointed to supersede Caesar.

In the confusion of the debates and votes in the Senate at Rome before Caesar crossed the Rubicon, one decree had been passed deposing him from his command of the army, and appointing a successor. The name of the general thus appointed was Domitius. The only real opposition which Caesar encountered in his progress toward Rome was from him. Domitius had crossed the Apennines at the head of an army on his way northward to supersede Caesar in his command, and had reached the town of Corfinium, which was perhaps one third of the way between Rome and the Rubicon. Caesar advanced upon him here and shut him in.

Caesar's treatment of Domitius.

After a brief siege the city was taken, and Domitius and his army were made prisoners. Every body gave them up for lost, expecting that Caesar would wreak terrible vengeance upon them. Instead of this, he received the troops at once into his own service, and let Domitius go free.

Dismay at Rome.

Pompey's distress.

In the mean time, the tidings of Caesar's having passed the Rubicon, and of the triumphant success which he was meeting with at the commencement of his march toward Rome, reached the Capitol, and added greatly to the prevailing consternation. The reports of the magnitude of his force and of the rapidity of his progress were greatly exaggerated. The party of Pompey and the Senate had done every thing to spread among the people the terror of Caesar's name, in order to arouse them to efforts for opposing his designs; and now, when he had broken through the barriers which had been intended to restrain him, and was advancing toward the city in an unchecked and triumphant career, they were overwhelmed with dismay. Pompey began to be terrified at the danger which was impending. The Senate held meetings without the city--councils of war, as it were, in which they looked to Pompey in vain for protection from the danger which he had brought upon them. He had said that he could raise an army sufficient to cope with Caesar at any time by stamping with his foot. They told him they thought now that it was high time for him to stamp.

He leaves Rome.

In fact, Pompey found the current setting every where strongly against him. Some recommended that commissioners should be sent to Caesar to make proposals for peace. The leading men, however, knowing that any peace made with him under such circumstances would be their own ruin, resisted and defeated the proposal. Cato abruptly left the city and proceeded to

Sicily, which had been assigned him as his province. Others fled in other directions. Pompey himself, uncertain what to do, and not daring to remain, called upon all his partisans to join him, and set off at night, suddenly, and with very little preparation and small supplies, to retreat across the country toward the shores of the Adriatic Sea, His destination was Brundusium, the usual port of embarkation for Macedon and Greece.

Enthusiasm of Caesar's soldiers.

Caesar was all this time gradually advancing toward Rome. His soldiers were full of enthusiasm in his cause. As his connection with the government at home was sundered the moment he crossed the Rubicon, all supplies of money and of provisions were cut off in that quarter until he should arrive at the Capitol and take possession of it. The soldiers voted, however, that they would serve him without pay. The officers, too, assembled together, and tendered him the aid of their contributions. He had always observed a very generous policy in his dealings with them, and he was now greatly gratified at receiving their requital of it.

His policy in releasing Domitius.

The further he advanced, too, the more he found the people of the country through which he passed disposed to espouse his cause. They were struck with his generosity in releasing Domitius. It is true that it was a very sagacious policy that prompted him to release him. But then it was generosity too. In fact, there must be something of a generous spirit in the soul to enable a man even to see the policy of generous actions.

Letter of Caesar.

Among the letters of Caesar that remain to the present day, there is one written about this time to one of his friends, in which he speaks of this subject. "I am glad," says he, "that you approve of my conduct at Corfinium. I am satisfied that such a course is the best one for us to pursue, as by so doing we shall gain the good will of all parties, and thus secure a permanent victory. Most conquerors have incurred the hatred of mankind by their cruelties, and have all, in consequence of the enmity they have thus awakened, been prevented from long enjoying their power. Sylla was an exception; but his example of successful cruelty I have no disposition to imitate. I will conquer after a new fashion, and fortify myself in the possession of the power I acquire by generosity and mercy."

Ingratitude of Domitius.

Domitius had the ingratitude, after this release, to take up arms again, and wage a new war against Caesar. When Caesar heard of it, he said it was all right. "I will act out the principles of my nature," said he, "and he may act out his."

Caesar's generosity.

Another instance of Caesar's generosity occurred, which is even more remarkable than this. It seems that among the officers of his army there were some whom he had appointed at the recommendation of Pompey, at the time when he and Pompey were friends. These men would, of course, feel under obligations of gratitude to Pompey, as they owed their military rank to his friendly interposition in their behalf. As soon as the war broke out, Caesar gave them all his free permission to go over to Pompey's side, if they chose to do so.

Modern politicians.

Caesar acted thus very liberally in all respects. He surpassed Pompey very much in the spirit of generosity and mercy with which he entered upon the great contest before them. Pompey ordered every citizen to join his standard, declaring that he should consider all neutrals as his enemies. Caesar, on the other hand, gave free permission to every one to decline, if he chose, taking any part in the contest, saying that he should consider all who did not act against him as his friends. In the political contests of our day, it is to be observed that the combatants are much more prone to imitate the bigotry of Pompey than the generosity of Caesar, condemning, as they often do, those who choose to stand aloof from electioneering struggles, more than they do their most determined opponents and enemies.

Caesar arrives at Brundusium.

When, at length, Caesar arrived at Brundusium, he found that Pompey had sent a part of his army across the Adriatic into Greece, and was waiting for the transports to return that he might go over himself with the remainder. In the mean time, he had fortified himself strongly in the city. Caesar immediately laid siege to the place, and he commenced some works to block up the mouth of the harbor. He built piers on each side, extending out as far into the sea as the depth of the water would allow them to be built. He then constructed a series of rafts, which he anchored on the deep water, in a line extending from one pier to the other. He built towers upon these rafts, and garrisoned them with soldiers, in hopes by this means to prevent all egress from the fort. He thought that, when this work was completed, Pompey would be entirely shut in, beyond all possibility of escape.

He besieges Pompey.

Pompey's plan of escape.

The transports, however, returned before the work was completed. Its progress was, of course, slow, as the constructions were the scene of a continued conflict; for Pompey sent out rafts and galleys against them every day, and the workmen had thus to build in the midst of continual interruptions, sometimes from showers of darts, arrows, and javelins, sometimes from the conflagrations of fireships, and sometimes from the terrible concussions of great vessels of war, impelled with prodigious force against them. The transports returned, therefore, before the defenses were complete, and contrived to get into the harbor. Pompey immediately formed his plan for embarking the remainder of his army.

It is made known to Caesar.

Success of Pompey's plan.

He filled the streets of the city with barricades and pitfalls, excepting two streets which led to the place of embarkation. The object of these obstructions was to embarrass Caesar's progress through the city in case he should force an entrance while his men were getting on board the ships. He then, in order to divert Caesar's attention from his design, doubled the guards stationed upon the walls on the evening of his intended embarkation, and ordered them to make vigorous attacks upon all Caesar's forces outside. He then, when the darkness came on, marched his troops through the two streets which had been left open, to the landing place, and got them as fast as possible on board the transports. Some of the people of the town contrived to make known to Caesar's army what was going on, by means of signals from the walls; the army immediately brought scaling ladders in great numbers, and, mounting the walls with great ardor and impetuosity, they drove all before them, and soon broke open the gates and got possession of the city. But the barricades and pitfalls, together with the darkness, so embarrassed their movements, that Pompey succeeded in completing his embarkation and sailing away.

Caesar's conduct at Rome.

Caesar had no ships in which to follow. He returned to Rome. He met, of course, with no opposition. He re-established the government there, organized the Senate anew, and obtained supplies of corn from the public granaries, and of money from the city treasury in the Capitol. In going to the Capitoline Hill after this treasure, he found the officer who had charge of the money stationed there to defend it. He told Caesar that it was contrary to law for him to enter. Caesar said that, for men with swords in their hands, there was no law. The officer still refused to admit him. Caesar then told him to open the doors, or he would kill him on the spot. "And you must understand," he added, "that it will be easier for me to do it than it has been to say it." The officer resisted no longer, and Caesar went in.

Caesar subdues various countries.

He turns his thoughts to Pompey.

After this, Caesar spent some time in rigorous campaigns in Italy, Spain, Sicily, and Gaul, wherever there was manifested any opposition to his sway. When this work was accomplished, and all these countries were completely subjected to his dominion, he began to turn his thoughts to the plan of pursuing Pompey across the Adriatic Sea.

## CHAPTER VII.: THE BATTLE OF PHARSALIA.

The gathering armies.

Pompey's preparations.

Caesar at Brundusium.

The gathering of the armies of Caesar and Pompey on the opposite shores of the Adriatic Sea was one of the grandest preparations for conflict that history has recorded, and the whole world gazed upon the spectacle at the time with an intense and eager interest, which was heightened by the awe and terror which the danger inspired. During the year while Caesar had been completing his work of subduing and arranging all the western part of the empire, Pompey had been gathering from the eastern division every possible contribution to swell the military force under his command, and had been concentrating all these elements of power on the coasts of Macedon and Greece, opposite to Brundusium, where he knew that Caesar would attempt to cross the Adriatic Sea, His camps, his detachments, his troops of archers and slingers, and his squadrons of horse, filled the land, while every port was guarded, and the line of the coast was environed by batteries and castles on the rocks, and fleets of galleys on the water. Caesar advanced with his immense army to Brundusium, on the opposite shore, in December, so that, in addition to the formidable resistance prepared for him by his enemy on the coast, he had to encounter the wild surges of the Adriatic, rolling perpetually in the dark and gloomy commotion always raised in such wide seas by wintery storms.

His address to his army.

Caesar had no ships, for Pompey had cleared the seas of every thing which could aid him in his intended passage. By great efforts, however, he succeeded at length in getting together a sufficient number of galleys to convey over a part of his army, provided he took the men alone, and left all his military stores and baggage behind. He gathered his army together, therefore, and made them an address, representing that they were now drawing toward the end of all their dangers and toils. They were about to meet their great enemy for a final conflict. It was not necessary to take their servants, their baggage, and their stores across the sea, for they were sure of victory, and victory would furnish them with ample supplies from those whom they were about to conquer.

Caesar crosses the Adriatic.

The soldiers eagerly imbibed the spirit of confidence and courage which Caesar himself expressed. A large detachment embarked and put to sea, and, after being tossed all night upon the cold and stormy waters, they approached the shore at some distance to the northward of the place where Pompey's fleets had expected them. It was at a point where the mountains came down near to the sea, rendering the coast rugged and dangerous with shelving rocks and frowning promontories. Here Caesar succeeded in effecting a landing of the first division of his troops, and then sent back the fleet for the remainder.

He subdues several towns.

Caesar's advance.

Distress of the armies.

The news of his passage spread rapidly to all Pompey's stations along the coast, and the ships began to gather, and the armies to march toward the point where Caesar had effected his landing. The conflict and struggle commenced. One of Pompey's admirals intercepted the fleet of galleys on their return, and seized and burned a large number of them, with all who were on board. This, of course, only renewed the determined desperation of the remainder. Caesar advanced along the coast with the troops which he had landed, driving Pompey's troops before him, and subduing town after town as he advanced. The country was filled with terror and dismay. The portion of the army which Caesar had left behind could not now cross, partly on account of the stormy condition of the seas, the diminished number of the ships, and the redoubled vigilance with which Pompey's forces now guarded the shores, but mainly because Caesar was now no longer with them to inspire them with his reckless, though calm and quiet daring. They remained, therefore, in anxiety and distress, on the Italian shore. As Caesar, on the other hand, advanced along the Macedonian shore, and drove Pompey back into the interior, he cut off the communication between Pompey's ships and the land, so that the fleet was soon reduced to great distress for want of provisions and water. The men kept themselves from perishing with thirst by collecting the dew which fell upon the decks of their galleys. Caesar's army was also in distress, for Pompey's fleets cut off all supplies by water, and his troops hemmed them in on the side of the land; and, lastly, Pompey himself, with the immense army that was under his command, began to be struck with alarm at the impending danger with which they were threatened. Pompey little realized, however, how dreadful a fate was soon to overwhelm him.

Caesar's impatience.

He attempts to cross the Adriatic.

The winter months rolled away, and nothing effectual was done. The forces, alternating and intermingled, as above described, kept each other in a continued state of anxiety and suffering. Caesar became impatient at the delay of that portion of his army that he had left on the Italian shore. The messages of encouragement and of urgency which he sent across to them did not bring them over, and at length, one dark and stormy night, when he thought that the inclemency of the skies and the heavy surging of the swell in the offing would drive his vigilant enemies into places of shelter, and put them off their guard, he determined to cross the sea himself and bring his hesitating army over. He ordered a galley to be prepared, and went on board of it disguised, and with his head muffled in his mantle, intending that not even the officers or crew of the ship which was to convey him should know of his design. The galley, in obedience to orders, put off from the shore. The mariners endeavored in vain for some time to make head against the violence of the wind and the heavy concussions of the waves, and at length, terrified at the imminence of the danger to which so wild and tumultuous a sea on such a night exposed them, refused to proceed, and the commander gave them orders to return. Caesar then came forward, threw off his mantle, and said to them, "Friends! you have nothing to fear. You are carrying Caesar."

The men were, of course, inspirited anew by this disclosure, but all was in vain. The obstacles to the passage proved insurmountable, and the galley, to avoid certain destruction, was compelled to return.

Caesar lands the remainder of his army.

The army, however, on the Italian side, hearing of Caesar's attempt to return to them, fruitless though it was, and stimulated by the renewed urgency of the orders which he now sent to them, made arrangements at last for an embarkation, and, after encountering great dangers on the way, succeeded in landing in safety. Caesar, thus strengthened, began to plan more decided operations for the coming spring.

Attempts at negotiation.

Conferences.

End in violence and disorder.

There were some attempts at negotiation. The armies were so exasperated against each other on account of the privations and hardships which each compelled the other to suffer, that they felt too strong a mutual distrust to attempt any regular communication by commissioners or ambassadors appointed for the purpose. They came to a parley, however, in one or two instances, though the interviews led to no result. As the missiles used in those days were such as could only be thrown to a very short distance, hostile bodies of men could approach much nearer to each other then than is possible now, when projectiles of the most terribly destructive character can be thrown for miles. In one instance, some of the ships of Pompey's fleet approached so near to the shore as to open a conference with one or two of Caesar's lieutenants who were encamped there. In another case, two bodies of troops from the respective armies were separated only by a river, and the officers and soldiers came down to the banks on either side, and held frequent conversations, calling to each other in loud voices across the water. In this way they succeeded in so far coming to an agreement as to fix upon a time and place for a more formal conference, to be held by commissioners chosen on each side. This conference was thus held, but each party came to it accompanied by a considerable body of attendants, and these, as might have been anticipated, came into open collision while the discussion was pending; thus the meeting consequently ended in violence and disorder, each party accusing the other of violating the faith which both had plighted.

Undecided warfare.

Bread made of roots.

This slow and undecided mode of warfare between the two vast armies continued for many months without any decisive results. There were skirmishes, struggles, sieges, blockades, and many brief and partial conflicts, but no general and decided battle. Now the advantage seemed on one side, and now on the other. Pompey so hemmed in Caesar's troops at one period, and so cut off his supplies, that the men were reduced to extreme distress for food. At length they found a kind of root which they dug from the ground, and, after drying and pulverizing it, they made a sort of bread of the powder, which the soldiers were willing to eat rather than either starve or give up the contest. They told Caesar, in fact, that they would live on the bark of trees rather than abandon his cause. Pompey's soldiers, at one time, coming near to the walls of a town which they occupied, taunted and jeered them on account of their wretched destitution of food. Caesar's soldiers threw loaves of this bread at them in return, by way of symbol that they were abundantly supplied.

Caesar hems Pompey in.

Anxiety of the rivals.

After some time the tide of fortune turned Caesar contrived, by a succession of adroit maneuvers and movements, to escape from his toils, and to circumvent and surround Pompey's forces so as soon to make them suffer destitution and distress in their turn. He cut off all communication between them and the country at large, and turned away the brooks and streams from flowing through the ground they occupied. An army of forty or fifty thousand men, with the immense number of horses and beasts of burden which accompany them, require very large supplies of water, and any destitution or even scarcity of water leads immediately to the most dreadful consequences. Pompey's troops dug wells, but they obtained only very insufficient supplies. Great numbers of beasts of burden died, and their decaying bodies so tainted the air as to produce epidemic diseases, which destroyed many of the troops, and depressed and disheartened those whom they did not destroy.

Nature of the contest between Caesar and Pompey.

Both hesitate.

During all these operations there was no decisive general battle. Each one of the great rivals knew very well that his defeat in one general battle would be his utter and irretrievable ruin. In a war between two independent nations, a single victory, however complete, seldom terminates the struggle, for the defeated party has the resources of a whole realm to fall back upon, which are sometimes called forth with renewed vigor after experiencing such reverses; and then defeat in such cases, even if it be final, does not necessarily involve the ruin of the unsuccessful commander. He may negotiate an honorable peace, and return to his own land in safety; and, if his misfortunes are considered by his countrymen as owing not to any dereliction from his duty as a soldier, but to the influence of adverse circumstances which no human skill or resolution could have controlled, he may spend the remainder of his days in prosperity and honor. The contest, however, between Caesar and Pompey was not of this character. One or the other of them was a traitor and a usurper--an enemy to his country. The result of a battle would decide which of the two was to stand in this attitude. Victory would legitimize and confirm the authority of one, and make it supreme over the whole civilized world. Defeat was to annihilate the power of the other, and make him a fugitive and a vagabond, without friends, without home, without country. It was a desperate stake; and it is not at all surprising that both parties lingered and hesitated, and postponed the throwing of the die.

The armies enter Thessaly.

At length Pompey, rendered desperate by the urgency of the destitution and distress into which Caesar had shut him, made a series of rigorous and successful attacks upon Caesar's lines, by which he broke away in his turn from his enemy's grasp, and the two armies moved slowly back into the interior of the country, hovering in the vicinity of each other, like birds of prey contending in the air, each continually striking at the other, and moving onward at the same time to gain some position of advantage, or to circumvent the other in such a design. They passed on in this manner over plains, and across rivers, and through mountain passes, until at length they reached the heart of Thessaly. Here at last the armies came to a stand and fought the final battle.

ROMAN STANDARD BEARERS.

The plain of Pharsalia.

Roman standard bearers.

Pompey draws up his army.

Forces on both sides.

The place was known then as the plain of Pharsalia, and the greatness of the contest which was decided there has immortalized its name. Pompey's forces were far more numerous than those of Caesar, and the advantage in all the partial contests which had taken place for some time had been on his side; he felt, consequently, sure of victory. He drew up his men in a line, one flank resting upon the bank of a river, which protected them from attack on that side. From this point, the long line of legions, drawn up in battle array, extended out upon the plain, and was terminated at the other extremity by strong squadrons of horse, and bodies of slingers and archers, so as to give the force of weapons and the activity of men as great a range as possible there, in order to prevent Caesar's being able to outflank and surround them There was, however, apparently very little danger of this, for Caesar, according to his own story, had but about half as strong a force as Pompey. The army of the latter, he says, consisted of nearly fifty thousand men, while his own number was between twenty and thirty thousand. Generals, however, are prone to magnify the military grandeur of their exploits by overrating the strength with which they had to contend, and under-estimating their own. We are therefore to receive with some distrust the statements made by Caesar and his partisans; and as for Pompey's story, the total and irreparable ruin in which he himself and all who adhered to him were entirely overwhelmed immediately after the battle, prevented its being ever told.

Appearance of Pompey's camp.

Pompey's tent.

In the rear of the plain where Pompey's lines were extended was the camp from which the army had been drawn out to prepare for the battle. The camp fires of the preceding night were moldering away, for it was a warm summer morning; the intrenchments were guarded, and the tents, now nearly empty, stood extended in long rows within the inclosure. In the midst of them was the magnificent pavilion of the general, furnished with every imaginable article of luxury and splendor. Attendants were busy here and there, some rearranging what had been left in disorder by the call to arms by which the troops had been summoned from their places of rest, and others providing refreshments-and food for their victorious comrades when they should return from the battle. In Pompey's tent a magnificent entertainment was preparing. The tables were spread with every luxury, the sideboards were loaded with plate, and the whole scene was resplendent with utensils and decorations of silver and gold.

His confidence of victory.

Pompey and all his generals were perfectly certain of victory. In fact, the peace and harmony of their councils in camp had been destroyed for many days by their contentions and disputes about the disposal of the high offices, and the places of profit and power at Rome, which were to come into their hands when Caesar should have been subdued. The subduing of Caesar they considered only a question of time; and, as a question of time, it was now reduced to very narrow limits. A few days more, and they were to be masters of the whole Roman empire, and, impatient and greedy, they disputed in anticipation about the division of the spoils.

To make assurance doubly sure, Pompey gave orders that his troops should not advance to meet the onset of Caesar's troops on the middle ground between the two armies, but that they should wait calmly for the attack, and receive the enemy at the posts where they had themselves been arrayed.

The battle of Pharsalia.

Defeat of Pompey.

Scene of horror.

The hour at length arrived, the charge was sounded by the trumpets, and Caesar's troops began to advance with loud shouts and great impetuosity toward Pompey's lines. There was a long and terrible struggle, but the forces of Pompey began finally to give way. Notwithstanding the precautions which Pompey had taken to guard and protect the wing of his army which was extended toward the land, Caesar succeeded in turning his flank upon that side by driving off the cavalry and destroying the archers and slingers, and he was thus enabled to throw a strong force upon Pompey's rear. The flight then soon became general, and a scene of dreadful confusion and slaughter ensued. The soldiers of Caesar's army, maddened with the insane rage which the progress of a battle never fails to awaken, and now excited to phrensy by the exultation of success, pressed on after the affrighted fugitives, who trampled one upon another, or fell pierced with the weapons of their assailants, filling the air with their cries of agony and their shrieks of terror. The horrors of the scene, far from allaying, only excited still more the ferocity of their bloodthirsty foes, and they pressed steadily and fiercely on, hour after hour, in their dreadful work of destruction. It was one of those scenes of horror and woe such as those who have not witnessed them can not conceive of, and those who have witnessed can never forget.

Pompey's flight to the camp.

Pompey in his tent.

His consternation and despair.

When Pompey perceived that all was lost, he fled from the field in a state of the wildest excitement and consternation. His troops were flying in all directions, some toward the camp, vainly hoping to find refuge there, and others in various other quarters, wherever they saw the readiest hope of escape from their merciless pursuers. Pompey himself fled instinctively toward the camp. As he passed the guards at the gate where he entered, he commanded them, in his agitation and terror, to defend the gate against the coming enemy, saying that he was going to the other gates to attend to the defenses there. He then hurried on, but a full sense of the helplessness and hopelessness of his condition soon overwhelmed him; he gave up all thought of defense, and, passing with a sinking heart through the scene of consternation and confusion which reigned every where within the encampment, he sought his own tent, and, rushing into it, sank down, amid the luxury and splendor which had been arranged to do honor to his anticipated victory, in a state of utter stupefaction and despair.

## CHAPTER VIII.: FLIGHT AND DEATH OF POMPEY.

Pursuit of the vanquished.

Pompey recovers himself.

Caesar pursued the discomfited and flying bodies of Pompey's army to the camp. They made a brief stand upon the ramparts and at the gates in a vain and fruitless struggle against the tide of victory which they soon perceived must fully overwhelm them. They gave way continually here and there along the lines of intrenchment, and column after column of Caesar's followers broke through into the camp. Pompey, hearing from his tent the increasing noise and uproar, was at length aroused from his stupor, and began to summon his faculties to the question what he was to do. At length a party of fugitives, hotly pursued by some of Caesar's soldiers, broke into his tent. "What!" said Pompey, "into my tent too!" He had been for more than thirty years a victorious general, accustomed to all the deference and respect which boundless wealth, extended and absolute power, and the highest military rank could afford. In the encampments which he had made, and in the cities which he had occupied from time to time, he had been the supreme and unquestioned master, and his tent, arranged and furnished, as it had always been, in a style of the utmost magnificence and splendor, had been sacred from all intrusion, and invested with such a dignity that potentates and princes were impressed when they entered, with a feeling of deference and awe. Now, rude soldiers burst wildly into it, and the air without was filled with an uproar and confusion, drawing every moment nearer and nearer, and warning the fallen hero that there was no longer any protection there against the approaching torrent which was coming on to overwhelm him.

Pompey disguises himself.

He escapes from the camp.

Pompey aroused himself from his stupor, threw off the military dress which belonged to his rank and station, and assumed a hasty disguise, in which he hoped he might make his escape from the immediate scene of his calamities. He mounted a horse and rode out of the camp at the easiest place of egress in the rear, in company with bodies of troops and guards who were also flying in confusion, while Caesar and his forces on the other side were carrying the intrenchments and forcing their way in. As soon is he had thus made his escape from the immediate scene of danger, he dismounted and left his horse, that he might assume more completely the appearance of a common soldier, and, with a few attendants who were willing to follow his fallen fortunes, he went on to the eastward, directing his weary steps toward the shores of the Aegean Sea.

The Vale of Tempe.

Its picturesqueness.

Pompey's sufferings.

A drink of water.

The country through which he was traveling was Thessaly. Thessaly is a vast amphitheater, surrounded by mountains, from whose sides streams descend, which, after watering many fertile valleys and plains, combine to form one great central river that flows to the eastward, and after various meanderings, finds its way into the Aegean Sea through a romantic gap between two mountains, called the Vale of Tempe--a vale which has been famed in all ages for the extreme picturesqueness of its scenery, and in which, in those days, all the charms both of the most alluring beauty and of the sublimest grandeur seemed to be combined. Pompey followed the roads leading along the banks of this stream, weary in body, and harassed and disconsolate in mind. The news which came to him from time to time, by the flying parties which were moving through the country in all directions, of the entire and overwhelming completeness of Caesar's victory, extinguished all remains of hope, and narrowed down at last the grounds of his solicitude to the single point of his own personal safety. He was well aware that he should be pursued, and, to baffle the efforts which he knew that his enemies would make to follow his track, he avoided large towns, and pressed forward in by-ways and solitudes, bearing as patiently as he was able his increasing destitution and distress. He reached, at length, the Vale of Tempe, and there, exhausted with hunger, thirst, and fatigue, he sat down upon the bank of the stream to recover by a little rest strength enough for the remainder of his weary way. He wished for a drink, but he had nothing to drink from. And so the mighty potentate, whose tent was full of delicious beverages, and cups and goblets of silver and gold, extended himself down upon the sand at the margin of the river, and drank the warm water directly from the stream.

Caesar in Pompey's camp.

While Pompey was thus anxiously and toilsomely endeavoring to gain the sea-shore, Caesar was completing his victory over the army which he had left behind him. When Caesar had carried the intrenchments of the camp, and the army found that there was no longer any safety for them there, they continued their retreat under the guidance of such generals as remained. Caesar thus gained undisputed possession of the camp. He found every where the marks of wealth and luxury, and indications of the confident expectation of victory which the discomfited army had entertained. The tents of the generals were crowned with myrtle, the beds were strewed with flowers, and tables every where were spread for feasts, with cups and bowls of wine all ready for the expected revelers. Caesar took possession of the whole, stationed a proper guard to protect the property, and then pressed forward with his army in pursuit of the enemy.

Retreat of Pompey's army.

Surrender of Pompey's army.

Pompey's army made their way to a neighboring rising ground, where they threw up hasty intrenchments to protect themselves for the night. A rivulet ran near the hill, the access to which they endeavored to secure, in order to obtain supplies of water. Caesar and his forces followed them to this spot. The day was gone, and it was too late to attack them. Caesar's soldiers, too, were exhausted with the intense and protracted excitement and exertions which had now been kept up for many hours in the battle and in the pursuit, and they needed repose. They made, however, one effort more. They seized the avenue of approach to the rivulet, and threw up a temporary intrenchment to secure it which intrenchment they protected with a guard; and then the army retired to rest, leaving their helpless victims to while away the hours of the night, tormented with thirst, and overwhelmed with anxiety and despair. This could not long be endured. They surrendered in the morning, and Caesar found himself in possession of over twenty thousand prisoners.

Pompey in the Vale of Tempe.

In the mean time, Pompey passed on through the Vale of Tempe toward the sea, regardless of the beauty and splendor that surrounded him, and thinking only of his fallen fortunes, and revolving despairingly in his mind the various forms in which the final consummation of his ruin might ultimately come. At length he reached the sea-shore, and found refuge for the night in a fisherman's cabin. A small number of attendants remained with him, some of whom were slaves. These he now dismissed, directing them to return and surrender themselves to Caesar, saying that he was a generous foe, and that they had nothing to fear from him. His other attendants he retained, and he made arrangements for a boat to take him the next day along the coast. It was a river boat, and unsuited to the open sea, but it was all that he could obtain.

Pompey embarks on board a vessel.

The shipmaster's dream.

He arose the next morning at break of day, and embarked in the little vessel, with two or three attendants, and the oarsmen began to row away along the shore. They soon came in sight of a merchant ship just ready to sail. The master of this vessel, it happened, had seen Pompey, and knew his countenance, and he had dreamed, as a famous historian of the times relates, on the night before, that Pompey had come to him hi the guise of a simple soldier and in great distress, and that he had received and rescued him. There was nothing extraordinary in such a dream at such a time, as the contest between Caesar and Pompey, and the approach of the final collision which was to destroy one or the other of them, filled the minds and occupied the conversation of the world. The shipmaster, therefore, having seen and known one of the great rivals in the approaching conflict, would naturally find both his waking and sleeping thoughts dwelling on the subject; and his fancy, in his dreams, might easily picture the scene of his rescuing and saving the fallen hero in the hour of his distress.

Pompey goes on board a merchant ship.

However this may be, the shipmaster is said to have been relating his dream to the seamen on the deck of his vessel when the boat which was conveying Pompey came into view. Pompey himself, having escaped from the land, supposed all immediate danger over, not imagining that seafaring men would recognize him in such a situation and in such a disguise. The shipmaster did, however, recognize him. He was overwhelmed with grief at seeing him in such a condition. With a countenance and with gestures expressive of earnest surprise and sorrow, he beckoned to Pompey to come on board. He ordered his own ship's boat to be immediately let down to meet and receive him. Pompey came on board. The ship was given up to his possession, and every possible arrangement was made to supply his wants, to contribute to his comfort, and to do him honor.

His arrival at Amphipolis.

The vessel conveyed him to Amphipolis, a city of Macedonia near the sea, and to the northward and eastward of the place where he had embarked. When Pompey arrived at the port he sent proclamations to the shore, calling upon the inhabitants to take arms and join his standard. He did not, however, land, or take any other measures for carrying these arrangements into effect. He only waited in the river upon which Amphipolis stands long enough to receive a supply of money from some of his friends on the shore, and stores for his voyage, and then get sail again. Whether he learned that Caesar was advancing in that direction with a force too strong for him to encounter, or found that the people were disinclined to espouse his cause, or whether the whole movement was a feint to direct Caesar's attention to Macedon as the field of his operations, in order that he might escape more secretly and safely beyond the sea, can not now be ascertained.

Pompey's wife Cornelia.

Her beauty and accomplishments.

Pompey's wife Cornelia was on the island of Lesbos, at Mitylene, near the western coast of Asia Minor. She was a lady of distinguished beauty, and of great intellectual superiority and moral worth. She was extremely well versed in all the learning of the times, and yet was entirely free from those peculiarities and airs which, as her historian says, were often observed in learned ladies in those days. Pompey had married her after the death of Julia, Caesar's daughter. They were strongly devoted to each other. Pompey had provided for her a beautiful retreat on the island of Lesbos, where she was living in elegance and splendor, beloved for her own intrinsic charms, and highly honored on account of the greatness and fame of her husband. Here she had received from time to time glowing accounts of his success all exaggerated as they came to her, through the eager desire of the narrators to give her pleasure.

Pompey's arrival at Mitylene.

His meeting with Cornelia.

From this high elevation of honor and happiness the ill-fated Cornelia suddenly fell, on the arrival of Pompey's solitary vessel at Mitylene, bringing as it did, at the same time, both the first intelligence of her husband's fall, and himself in person, a ruined and homeless fugitive and wanderer. The meeting was sad and sorrowful. Cornelia was overwhelmed at the suddenness and violence of the shock which it brought her, and Pompey lamented anew the dreadful disaster that he had sustained, at finding how inevitably it must involve his beloved wife as well as himself in its irreparable ruin.

Pompey gathers a little fleet.

The pain, however, was not wholly without some mingling of pleasure. A husband finds a strange sense of protection and safety in the presence and sympathy of an affectionate wife in the hour of his calamity. She can, perhaps do nothing, but her mute and sorrowful concern and pity comfort and reassure him. Cornelia, however, was able to render her husband some essential aid. She resolved immediately to accompany him wherever he should go; and, by their joint endeavors, a little fleet was gathered, and such supplies as could be hastily obtained, and such attendants and followers as were willing to share his fate, were taken on board. During all this time Pompey would not go on shore himself, but remained on board, his ship in the harbor.

Perhaps he was afraid of some treachery or surprise, or perhaps, in his fallen and hopeless condition, he was unwilling to expose himself to the gaze of those who had so often seen him in all the splendor of his former power.

He sails along the Mediterranean.

Pompey receives additional supplies.

At length, when all was ready, he sailed away. He passed eastward along the Mediterranean, touching at such ports as he supposed most likely to favor his cause. Vague and uncertain, but still alarming rumors that Caesar was advancing in pursuit of him met him every where, and the people of the various provinces were taking sides, some in his favor and some against him, the excitement being every where so great that the utmost caution and circumspection were required in all his movements. Sometimes he was refused permission to land; at others, his friends were too few to afford him protection; and at others still, though the authorities professed friendship, he did not dare to trust them. He obtained, however, some supplies of money and some accessions to the number of ships and men under his command, until at length he had quite a little fleet in his train. Several men of rank and influence, who had served under him in the days of his prosperity, nobly adhered to him now, and formed a sort of court or council on board his galley, where they held with their great though fallen commander frequent conversations on the plan which it was best to pursue.

He seeks refuge in Egypt.

Ptolemy and Cleopatra.

It was finally decided that it was best to seek refuge in Egypt. There seemed to be, in fact, no alternative. All the rest of the world was evidently going over to Caesar. Pompey had been the means, some years before, of restoring a certain king of Egypt to his throne, and many of his soldiers had been left in the country, and remained there still. It is true that the king himself had died. He had left a daughter named Cleopatra, and also a son, who was at this time very young. The name of this youthful prince was Ptolemy. Ptolemy and Cleopatra bad been made by their father joint heirs to the throne. But Ptolemy, or, rather, the ministers and counselors who acted for him and in his name, had expelled Cleopatra, that they might govern alone. Cleopatra had raised an army in Syria, and was on her way to the frontiers of Egypt to regain possession of what she deemed her rights. Ptolemy's ministers had gone forth to meet her at the head of their own troops, 'Ptolemy himself being also with them. They had reached Pelusium, which is the frontier town between Egypt and Syria on the coast of the Mediterranean. Here their armies had assembled in vast encampments upon the land, and their galleys and transports were riding at anchor along the shore of the sea. Pompey and his-counselors thought that the government of Ptolemy would receive him as a friend, on account of the services he had rendered to the young prince's father, forgetting that gratitude has never a place on the list of political virtues.

Pompey arrives at Pelusium.

Pompey's little squadron made its way slowly over the waters of the Mediterranean toward Pelusium and the camp of Ptolemy. As they approached the shore, both Pompey himself and Cornelia felt many anxious forebodings. A messenger was sent to the land to inform the young king of Pompey's approach, and to solicit his protection. The government of Ptolemy held a council, and took the subject into consideration.

Ptolemy's council resolve to murder Pompey.

Various opinions were expressed, and various plans were proposed. The counsel which was finally followed was this. It would be dangerous to receive Pompey, since that would make Caesar their enemy. It would be dangerous to refuse to receive him, as that would make Pompey their enemy, and, though powerless now, he might one day be in a condition to seek vengeance. It was wisest, therefore, to destroy him. They would invite him to the shore, and kill him when he landed. This would please Caesar; and Pompey himself, being dead, could never revenge it. "Dead dogs," as the orator said who made this atrocious proposal, "do not bite."

The assassin Achillas.

An Egyptian, named Achillas, was appointed to execute the assassination thus decreed. An invitation was sent to Pompey to land, accompanied with a promise of protection; and, when his fleet had approached near enough to the shore, Achillas took a small party in a boat, and went out to meet his galley. The men in this boat, of course, were armed.

Suspicions of Pompey's friends.

Entreaties of Cornelia.

Pompey's forlorn condition.

He determines to land.

The officers and attendants of Pompey watched all these movements from the deck of his galley. They scrutinized every thing that occurred with the closest attention and the greatest anxiety, to see whether the indications denoted an honest friendship or intentions of treachery. The appearances were not favorable. Pompey's friends observed that no preparations were making along the shore for receiving him with the honors due, as they thought, to his rank and station. The manner, too, in which the Egyptians seemed to expect him to land was ominous of evil. Only a single insignificant boat for a potentate who recently had commanded half the world! Then, besides, the friends of Pompey observed that several of the principal galleys of Ptolemy's fleet were getting up their anchors, and preparing apparently to be ready to move at a sudden call These and other indications appeared much more like preparations for seizing an enemy than welcoming a friend. Cornelia, who, with her little son, stood upon the deck of Pompey's galley, watching the scene with a peculiar intensity of solicitude which the hardy soldiers around her could not have felt, became soon exceedingly alarm ad. She begged her husband Dot to go on shore. But Pompey decided that it was now too late to retreat. He could not escape from the Egyptian galleys if they had received orders to intercept him, nor could he resist violence if violence were intended. To do any thing like that would evince distrust, and to appear like putting himself upon his guard would be to take at once, himself, the position of an enemy, and invite and justify the hostility of the Egyptians in return. As to flight, he could not hope to escape from the Egyptian galleys if they had received orders to prevent it; and, besides, if he were determined on attempting an escape, whither should he fly? The world was against him. His triumphant enemy was on his track in full pursuit, with all the vast powers and resources of the whole Roman empire at his command. There remained for Pompey only the last forlorn hope of a refuge in Egypt, or else, as the sole alternative, a complete and unconditional submission to Caesar. His pride would not consent to this, and he determined, therefore, dark as the indications were, to place himself, without any appearance of distrust, in Ptolemy's hands, and abide the issue.

The boat of Achillas approached the galley. When it touched the side, Achillas and the other officers on board of it hailed Pompey in the most respectful manner, giving him the title of Imperator, the highest title known in the Roman state. Achillas addressed Pompey in Greek. The Greek was the language of educated men in all the Eastern countries in those days. He told him that the water was too shallow for his galley to approach nearer to the shore, and invited him to come on board of his boat, and he would take him to the beach, where, as he said, the king was waiting to receive him.

Preparations for landing.

Pompey takes leave of his wife.

With many anxious forebodings, that were but ill concealed, Pompey made preparations to accept the invitation. He bade his wife farewell, who clung to him as they were about to part with a gloomy presentiment that they should never meet again. Two centurions who were to accompany Pompey, and two servants, descended into the boat. Pompey himself followed, and then the boatmen pushed off from the galley and made toward the shore. The decks of all the vessels in Pompey's little squadron, as well as those of the Egyptian fleet, were crowded with spectators, and lines of soldiery and groups of men, all intently watching the operations of the landing, were scattered along the shore.

The assassins.

Gloomy silence.

Among the men whom Achillas had provided to aid him in the assassination was an officer of the Roman army who had formerly served under Pompey. As soon as Pompey was seated in the boat, he recognized the countenance of this man, and addressed him, saying, "I think I remember you as having been in former days my fellow-soldier." The man replied merely by a nod of assent. Feeling somewhat guilty and self-condemned at the thoughts of the treachery which he was about to perpetrate, he was little inclined to renew the recollection of the days when he was Pompey's friend. In fact, the whole company in the boat, filled on the one part with awe in anticipation of the terrible deed which they were soon to commit, and on the other with a dread suspense and alarm, were little disposed for conversation, and Pompey took out a manuscript of an address in Greek which he had prepared to make to the young king at his approaching interview with him, and occupied himself in reading it over. Thus they advanced in a gloomy and solemn silence, hearing no sound but the dip of the oars in the water, and the gentle dash of the waves along the line of the shore.

Assassination of Pompey.

At length the boat touched the sand, while Cornelia still stood on the deck of the galley, watching every movement with great solicitude and concern. One of the two servants whom

Pompey had taken with him, named Philip, his favorite personal attendant, rose to assist his master in landing. He gave Pompey his hand to aid him in rising from his seat, and at that moment the Roman officer whom Pompey had recognized as his fellow-soldier, advanced behind him and stabbed him in the back. At the same instant Achillas and the others drew their swords. Pompey saw that all was lost. He did not speak, and he uttered no cry of alarm, though Cornelia's dreadful shriek was so loud and piercing that it was heard upon the shore. From the suffering victim himself nothing was heard but an inarticulate groan extorted by his agony. He gathered his mantle over his face, and sank down and died.

Cornelia.

The funeral pile.

Pompey's ashes sent to Cornelia.

Of course, all was now excitement and confusion. As soon as the deed was done, the perpetrators of it retired from the scene, taking the head of their unhappy victim with them, to offer to Caesar as proof that his enemy was really no more. The officers who remained in the fleet which had brought Pompey to the coast made all haste to sail away, bearing the wretched Cornelia with them, utterly distracted with grief and despair, while Philip and his fellow-servant remained upon the beach, standing bewildered and stupefied over the headless body of their beloved master. Crowds of spectators came in succession to look upon the hideous spectacle a moment in silence, and then to turn, shocked and repelled, away. At length, when the first impulse of excitement had in some measure spent its force, Philip and his comrades so far recovered their composure as to begin to turn their thoughts to the only consolation that was now left to them, that of performing the solemn duties of sepulture. They found the wreck of a fishing boat upon the strand, from which they obtained wood enough for a rude funeral pile. They burned what remained of the mutilated body, and, gathering up the ashes, they put them in an urn and sent them to Cornelia, who afterward buried them at Alba with many bitter tears.

Death of Pompey.

## CHAPTER IX.: CAESAR IN EGYPT.

Caesar after the battle of Pharsalia.

Caesar surveyed the field of battle after the victory of Pharsalia, not with the feelings of exultation which might have been expected in a victorious general, but with compassion and sorrow for the fallen soldiers whose dead bodies covered the ground. After gazing upon the scene sadly and in silence for a time, he said, "They would have it so," and thus dismissed from his mind all sense of his own responsibility for the consequences which had ensued.

His clemency.

Caesar pursues Pompey.

He treated the immense body of prisoners which had fallen into his hands with great clemency, partly from the natural impulses of his disposition, which were always generous and noble, and partly from policy, that he might conciliate them all, officers and soldiers, to acquiescence in his future rule. He then sent back a large portion of his force to Italy, and, taking a body of cavalry from the rest, in order that he might advance with the utmost possible rapidity, he set off through Thessaly and Macedon in pursuit of his fugitive foe.

Treasures of the Temple of Diana.

He had no naval force at his command, and he accordingly kept upon the land. Besides, he wished, by moving through the country at the head of an armed force, to make a demonstration which should put down any attempt that might be made in arty quarter to rally or concentrate a force in Pompey's favor. He crossed the Hellespont, and moved down the coast of Asia Minor. There was a great temple consecrated to Diana at Ephesus, which, for its wealth and magnificence, was then the wonder of the world. The authorities who had it in their charge, not aware of Caesar's approach, had concluded to withdraw the treasures from the temple and loan them to Pompey, to be repaid when he should have regained his Dower. An assembly was accordingly convened to witness the delivery of the treasures, and take note of their value, which ceremony was to be performed with great formality and parade, when they learned that Caesar had crossed the Hellespont and was drawing near. The whole proceeding was thus arrested, and the treasures were retained.

Caesar in Asia Minor.

He sails for Egypt.

Caesar passed rapidly on through Asia Minor, examining and comparing, as he advanced, the vague rumors which were continually coming in in respect to Pompey's movements. He learned at length that he had gone to Cyprus; he presumed that his destination was Egypt, and he immediately resolved to provide himself with a fleet, and follow him thither by sea. As time passed on, and the news of Pompey's defeat and flight, and of Caesar's triumphant pursuit of him, became generally extended and confirmed, the various powers ruling in all that region of the world abandoned one after another the hopeless cause, and began to adhere to Caesar. They offered him such resources and aid as he might desire. He did not, however, stop to organize a large fleet or to collect an army. He depended, like Napoleon, in all the great movements of his life, not on grandeur of preparation, but on celerity of action. He organized at Rhodes a small but very efficient fleet of ten galleys, and, embarking his best troops in them, he made sail for the coasts of Egypt. Pompey had landed at Pelusium, on the eastern frontier, having heard that the young king and his court were there to meet and resist Cleopatra's invasion. Caesar, however, with the characteristic boldness and energy of his character, proceeded directly to Alexandria, the capital.

Caesar at Alexandria.

Egypt was, in those days, an ally of the Romans, as the phrase was; that is, the country, though it preserved its independent organization and its forms of royalty, was still united to the Roman people by an intimate league, so as to form an integral part of the great empire. Caesar, consequently, in appearing there with an armed force, would naturally be received as a friend. He found only the garrison which Ptolemy's government had left in charge of the city. At first the officers of this garrison gave him an outwardly friendly reception, but they soon began to take offense at the air of authority and command which he assumed, and which seemed to them to indicate a spirit of encroachment on the sovereignty of their own king.

The Roman fasces.

The lictors.

Feelings of deeply-seated alienation and animosity sometimes find their outward expression in contests about things intrinsically of very little importance. It was so in this case. The Roman consuls were accustomed to use a certain badge of authority called the fasces. It consisted of a bundle of rods, bound around the handle of an ax. Whenever a consul appeared in public, he was preceded by two officers called lictors, each of whom carried the fasces as a symbol of the power which was vested in the distinguished personage who followed them.

The Egyptian officers and the people of the city quarreled with Caesar on account of his moving about among them in his imperial state, accompanied by a life guard, and preceded by the lictors. Contests occurred between his troops and those of the garrison, and many disturbances were created in the streets of the city. Although no serious collision took place, Caesar thought it prudent to strengthen his force, and he sent back to Europe for additional legions to come to Egypt and join him.

Pompey's head sent to Caesar.

Caesar mourns Pompey.

The tidings of Pompey's death came to Caesar at Alexandria, and with them the head of the murdered man, which was sent by the government of Ptolemy, they supposing that it would be an acceptable gift to Caesar. Instead of being pleased with it, Caesar turned from the shocking spectacle in horror. Pompey had been, for many years now gone by, Caesar's colleague and friend. He had been his son-in-law, and thus had sustained to him a very near and endearing relation. In the contest which had at last unfortunately arisen, Pompey had done no wrong either to Caesar or to the government at Rome. He was the injured party, so far as there was a right and a wrong to such a quarrel. And now, after being hunted through half the world by his triumphant enemy, he had been treacherously murdered by men pretending to receive him as a friend. The natural sense of justice, which formed originally so strong a trait in Caesar's character, was not yet wholly extinguished. He could not but feel some remorse at the thoughts of the long course of violence and wrong which he had pursued against his old champion and friend, and which had led at last to so dreadful an end. Instead of being pleased with the horrid trophy which the Egyptians sent him, he mourned the death of his great rival with sincere and unaffected grief, and was filled with indignation against his murderers.

Pompey's signet ring.

Caesar's respect for Pompey's memory.

Pompey's Pillar.

Origin of Pompey's Pillar.

Pompey's Pillar.

Pompey had a signet ring upon his finger at the time of his assassination, which was taken off by the Egyptian officers and carried away to Ptolemy, together with the other articles of value which had been found upon his person. Ptolemy sent this seal to Caesar to complete the proof that its possessor was no more. Caesar received this memorial with eager though mournful pleasure, and he preserved it with great care. And in many ways, during all the remainder of his life, he manifested every outward indication of cherishing the highest respect for Pompey's memory. There stands to the present day, among the ruins of Alexandria, a beautiful column, about one hundred feet high, which has been known in all modern times as POMPEY'S PILLAR. It is formed of stone, and is in three parts. One stone forms the pedestal, another the shaft, and a third the capital. The beauty of this column, the perfection of its workmanship, which still continues in excellent preservation, and its antiquity, so great that all distinct record of its origin is lost, have combined to make it for many ages the wonder and admiration of mankind. Although no history of its origin has come down to us, a tradition has descended that Caesar built it during his residence in Egypt, to commemorate the name of Pompey; but whether it was his own victory over Pompey, or Pompey's own character and military fame which the structure was intended to signalize to mankind, can not now be known. There is even some doubt whether it was erected by Caesar at all.

Surrender of Pompey's officers.

Caesar's generosity.

While Caesar was in Alexandria, many of Pompey's officers, now that their master was dead, and there was no longer any possibility of their rallying again under his guidance and command, came in and surrendered themselves to him. He received them with great kindness, and, instead of visiting them with any penalties for having fought against him, he honored the fidelity and bravery they had evinced in the service of their own former master. Caesar had, in fact, shown the same generosity to the soldiers of Pompey's army that he had taken prisoners at the battle of Pharsalia. At the close of the battle, he issued orders that each one of his soldiers should have permission to save one of the enemy. Nothing could more strikingly exemplify both the generosity and the tact that marked the great conqueror's character than this incident. The hatred and revenge which had animated his victorious soldiery in the battle and in the pursuit, were changed immediately by the permission to compassion and good will. The ferocious soldiers turned at once from the pleasure of hunting their discomfited enemies to death, to that of protecting and defending them; and the way was prepared for their being received into his service, and incorporated with the rest of his army as friends and brothers.

His position at Alexandria.

Caesar's interference in Egyptian affairs.

Caesar soon found himself in so strong a position at Alexandria, that he determined to exercise his authority as Roman consul to settle the dispute in respect to the succession of the Egyptian crown. There was no difficulty in finding pretexts for interfering in the affairs of Egypt. In the first place, there was, as he contended, great anarchy and confusion at Alexandria, people taking different sides in the controversy with such fierceness as to render it impossible that good government and public order should be restored until this great question was settled. He also claimed a debt due from the Egyptian government, which Photinus, Ptolemy's minister at Alexandria, was very dilatory in paying. This led to animosities and disputes; and, finally, Caesar found, or pretended to find, evidence that Photinus was forming plots against his life. At length Caesar determined on taking decided action. He sent orders both to Ptolemy and to Cleopatra to disband their forces, to repair to Alexandria, and lay their respective claims before him for his adjudication.

Cleopatra.

Cleopatra complied with this summons, and returned to Egypt with a view to submitting her case to Caesar's arbitration. Ptolemy determined to resist. He advanced toward Egypt, but it was at the head of his army, and with a determination to drive Caesar and all his Roman followers away.

Caesar's guilty passion for Cleopatra.

When Cleopatra arrived, she found that the avenues of approach to Caesar's quarters were all in possession of her enemies, so that, in attempting to join him, she incurred danger of falling into their hands as a prisoner. She resorted to a stratagem, as the story is, to gain a secret admission. They rolled her up in a sort of bale of bedding or carpeting, and she was carried in in this way on the back of a man, through the guards, who might otherwise have intercepted her. Caesar was very much pleased with this device, and with the successful result of it. Cleopatra, too, was young and beautiful, and Caesar immediately conceived a strong but guilty attachment to her, which she readily returned. Caesar espoused her cause, and decided that she and Ptolemy should jointly occupy the throne.

Resistance of Ptolemy.

The Alexandrine war.

Ptolemy and his partisans were determined not to submit to this award. The consequence was, a violent and protracted war. Ptolemy was not only incensed at being deprived of what he considered his just right to the realm, he was also half distracted at the thought of his sister's disgraceful connection with Caesar. His excitement and distress, and the exertions and efforts to which they aroused him, awakened a strong sympathy in his cause among the people, and Caesar found himself involved in a very serious contest, in which his own life was brought repeatedly into the most imminent danger, and which seriously threatened the total destruction of his power. He, however, braved all the difficulty and dangers, and recklessly persisted in the course he had taken, under the influence of the infatuation in which his attachment to Cleopatra held him, as by a spell.

The Pharos.

Great splendor of the Pharos.

The war in which Caesar was thus involved by his efforts to give Cleopatra a seat with her brother on the Egyptian throne, is called in history the Alexandrine war. It was marked by many strange and romantic incidents. There was a light-house, called the Pharos, on a small island opposite the harbor of Alexandria, and it was so famed, both on account of the great magnificence of the edifice itself, and also on account of its position at the entrance to the greatest commercial port in the world, that it has given its name, as a generic appellation, to all other structures of the kind--any light-house being now called a Pharos, just as any serious difficulty is called a Gordian knot. The Pharos was a lofty tower--the accounts say that it was five hundred feet in height, which would be an enormous elevation for such a structure--and in a lantern at the top a brilliant light was kept constantly burning, which could be seen over the water for a hundred miles. The tower was built in several successive stories, each being ornamented with balustrades, galleries, and columns, so that the splendor of the architecture by day rivaled the brilliancy of the radiation which beamed from the summit by night. Far and wide over the stormy waters of the Mediterranean this meteor glowed, inviting and guiding the mariners in; and both its welcome and its guidance were doubly prized in those ancient days, when there was neither compass nor sextant on which they could rely. In the course of the contest with the Egyptians, Caesar took possession of the Pharos, and of the island on which it stood; and as the Pharos was then regarded as one of the seven wonders of the world, the fame of the exploit, though it was probably nothing remarkable in a military point of view, spread rapidly throughout the world.

It is captured by Caesar.

And yet, though the capture of a light-house was no very extraordinary conquest, in the course of the contests on the harbor which were connected with it Caesar had a very narrow escape from death. In all such struggles he was accustomed always to take personally his full share of the exposure and the danger. This resulted in part from the natural impetuosity and ardor of his character, which were always aroused to double intensity of action by the excitement of battle, and partly from the ideas of the military duty of a commander which prevailed in those days. There was besides, in this case, an additional inducement to acquire the glory of extraordinary exploits, in Caesar's desire to be the object of Cleopatra's admiration, who watched all his movements, and who was doubly pleased with his prowess and bravery, since she saw that they were exercised for her sake and in her cause.

Situation of the Pharos.

Caesar's personal danger.

Caesar's narrow escape.

The Pharos was built upon an island, which was connected by a pier or bridge with the main land. In the course of the attack upon this bridge, Caesar, with a party of his followers, got driven back and hemmed in by a body of the enemy that surrounded them, in such a place that the only mode of escape seemed to be by a boat, which might take them to a neighboring galley. They began, therefore, all to crowd into the boat in confusion, and so overloaded it that it was obviously in imminent danger of being upset or of sinking. The upsetting or sinking of an overloaded boat brings almost certain destruction upon most of the passengers, whether swimmers or not, as they seize each other in their terror, and go down inextricably entangled together, each held by the others in the convulsive grasp with which drowning men always cling to whatever is within their reach. Caesar, anticipating this danger, leaped over into the sea and swam to the ship. He had some papers in his hand at the time--plans, perhaps, of the works which he was assailing. These he held above the water with his left hand, while he swam with the right. And to save his purple cloak or mantle, the emblem of his imperial dignity, which he supposed the enemy would eagerly seek to obtain as a trophy, he seized it by a corner between his teeth, and drew it after him through the water as he swam toward the galley. The boat which he thus escaped from soon after went down, with all on board.

The Alexandrian library.

Burning of the Alexandrian library.

During the progress of this Alexandrine war one great disaster occurred, which has given to the contest a most melancholy celebrity in all subsequent ages: this disaster was the destruction of the Alexandrian library. The Egyptians were celebrated for their learning, and, under the munificent patronage of some of their kings, the learned men of Alexandria had made an enormous collection of writings, which were inscribed, as was the custom in those days, on parchment rolls. The number of the rolls or volumes was said to be seven hundred thousand; and when we consider that each one was written with great care, in beautiful characters, with a pen, and at a vast expense, it is not surprising that the collection was the admiration of the world. In fact, the whole body of ancient literature was there recorded. Caesar set fire to some Egyptian galleys, which lay so near the shore that the wind blew the sparks and flames upon the buildings on the quay. The fire spread among the palaces and other magnificent edifices of that part of the city, and one of the great buildings in which the library was stored was reached and destroyed. There was no other such collection in the world; and the consequence of this calamity has been, that it is only detached and insulated fragments of ancient literature and science that have come down to our times. The world will never cease to mourn the irreparable loss.

Caesar returns to Rome.

Notwithstanding the various untoward incidents which attended the war in Alexandria during its progress, Caesar, as usual, conquered in the end. The young king Ptolemy was defeated, and, in attempting to make his escape across a branch of the Nile, he was drowned. Caesar then finally settled the kingdom upon Cleopatra and a younger brother, and, after remaining for some time longer in Egypt, he set out on his return to Rome.

Cleopatra's Barge.

Subsequent adventures of Cleopatra.

The subsequent adventures of Cleopatra were as romantic as to have given her name a very wide celebrity. The lives of the virtuous pass smoothly and happily away, but the tale, when told to others, possesses but little interest or attraction; while those of the wicked, whose days are spent in wretchedness and despair, and are thus full of misery to the actors themselves, afford to the rest of mankind a high degree of pleasure, from the dramatic interest of the story.

Her splendid barge.

Anthony and Octavius.

Death of Cleopatra.

Cleopatra led a life of splendid sin, and, of course, of splendid misery. She visited Caesar in Rome after his return thither. Caesar received her magnificently, and paid her all possible honors; but the people of Rome regarded her with strong reprobation. When her young brother, whom Caesar had made her partner on the throne, was old enough to claim his share, she poisoned him. After Caesar's death, she went from Alexandria to Syria to meet Antony, one of Caesar's successors, in a galley or barge, which was so rich, so splendid, so magnificently furnished and adorned, that it was famed throughout the world as Cleopatra's barge. A great many beautiful vessels have since been called by the same name. Cleopatra connected herself with Antony, who became infatuated with her beauty and her various charms as Caesar had been. After a great variety of romantic adventures, Antony was defeated in battle by his great rival Octavius, and, supposing that he had been betrayed by Cleopatra, he pursued her to Egypt, intending to kill her. She hid herself in a sepulcher, spreading a report that she had committed suicide, and then Antony stabbed himself in a fit of remorse and despair. Before he died, he learned that Cleopatra was alive, and he caused himself to be carried into her presence and died in her arms. Cleopatra then fell into the hands of Octavius, who intended to carry her to Rome to grace his triumph. To save herself from this humiliation, and weary with a life which, full of sin as it had been, was a constant series of sufferings, she determined to die. A servant brought in an asp for her, concealed in a vase of flowers, at a great banquet. She laid the poisonous reptile on her naked arm, and died immediately of the bite which it inflicted.

## CHAPTER X.: CAESAR IMPERATOR.

Caesar again at Rome.
Combinations against him.
Veni, vidi, vici.

Although Pompey himself had been killed, and the army under his immediate command entirely annihilated, Caesar did not find that the empire was yet completely submissive to his sway. As the tidings of his conquests spread over the vast and distant regions which were under the Roman rule--although the story itself of his exploits might have been exaggerated--the impression produced by his power lost something of its strength, as men generally have little dread of remote danger. While he was in Egypt, there were three great concentrations of power formed against him in other quarters of the globe: in Asia Minor, in Africa, and in Spain. In putting down these three great and formidable arrays of opposition, Caesar made an exhibition to the world of that astonishing promptness and celerity of military action on which his fame as a general so much depends. He went first to Asia Minor, and fought a great and decisive battle there, in a manner so sudden and unexpected to the forces that opposed him that they found themselves defeated almost before they suspected that their enemy was near. It was in reference to this battle that he wrote the inscription for the banner, "Veni, vidi, vici" The words may be rendered in English, "I came, looked, and conquered," though the peculiar force of the expression, as well as the alliteration, is lost in any attempt to translate it.

Caesar made dictator.

In the mean time, Caesar's prosperity and success had greatly strengthened his cause at Rome. Rome was supported in a great measure by the contributions brought home from the provinces by the various military heroes who were sent out to govern them; and, of course, the greater and more successful was the conqueror, the better was he qualified for stations of highest authority in the estimation of the inhabitants of the city. They made Caesar dictator even while he was away, and appointed Mark Antony his master of horse. This was the same Antony whom we have already mentioned as having been connected with Cleopatra after Caesar's death. Rome, in fact, was filled with the fame of Caesar's exploits, and, as he crossed the Adriatic and advanced toward the city, he found himself the object of universal admiration and applause.

Opposition of Cato.
Pompey's sons.

But he could not yet be contented to establish himself quietly at Rome. There was a large force organized against him in Africa under Cato, a stern and indomitable man, who had long been an enemy to Caesar, and who now considered him as a usurper and an enemy of the republic, and was determined to resist him to the last extremity. There was also a large force assembled in Spain under the command of two sons of Pompey, in whose case the ordinary political hostility of contending partisans was rendered doubly intense and bitter by their desire to avenge their father's cruel fate. Caesar determined first to go to Africa, and then, after disposing of Cato's resistance, to cross the Mediterranean into Spain.

Complaints of the soldiers.

Before he could set out, however, on these expeditions, he was involved in very serious difficulties for a time, on account of a great discontent which prevailed in his army, and which ended at last in open mutiny. The soldiers complained that they had not received the rewards and honors which Caesar had promised them. Some claimed offices, others money others lands, which, as they maintained, they had been led to expect would be conferred upon them at the end of the campaign. The fact undoubtedly was, that, elated with their success, and intoxicated with the spectacle of the boundless influence and power which their general so obviously wielded at Rome, they formed expectations and hopes for themselves altogether too wild and unreasonable to be realized by soldiers; for soldiers, however much they may be flattered by their generals in going into battle, or praised in the mass in official dispatches, are after all but slaves, and slaves, too, of the very humblest caste and character.

The mutiny.

The army marches to Rome.

The famous tenth legion, Cesar's favorite corps, took the most active part in fomenting these discontents, as might naturally have been expected, since the attentions and the praises which he had bestowed upon them, though at first they tended to awaken their ambition, and to inspire them with redoubled ardor and courage, ended, as such favoritism always does, in making them vain, self-important, and unreasonable. Led on thus by the tenth legion, the whole army mutinied. They broke up the camp where they had been stationed at some distance beyond the walls of Rome, and marched toward the city. Soldiers in a mutiny, even though headed by their subaltern officers, are very little under command; and these Roman troops, feeling released from their usual restraints, committed various excesses on the way, terrifying the inhabitants and spreading universal alarm. The people of the city were thrown into utter consternation at the approach of the vast horde, which was coming like a terrible avalanche to descend upon them.

Plan of the soldiers.

The army expected some signs of resistance at the gates, which, if offered, they were prepared to encounter and overcome. Their plan was, after entering the city, to seek Caesar and demand their discharge from his service. They knew that he was under the necessity of immediately making a campaign in Africa, and that, of course, he could not possibly, as they supposed, dispense with them. He would, consequently, if they asked their discharge, beg them to remain, and, to induce them to do it, would comply with all their expectations and desires.

Such was their plan. To tender, however, a resignation of an office as a means of bringing an opposite party to terms, is always a very hazardous experiment. We easily overrate the estimation in which our own services are held taking what is said to us in kindness or courtesy by friends as the sober and deliberate judgment of the public; and thus it often happens that persons who in such case offer to resign, are astonished to find their resignations readily accepted.

The army marches into the city.

When Caesar's mutineers arrived at the gates, they found, instead of opposition, only orders from Caesar, by which they were directed to leave all their arms except their swords, and march into the city. They obeyed. They were then directed to go to the Campus Martius, a vast parade ground situated within the walls, and to await Caesar's orders there.

The Campus Martius.

Caesar's address to the army.

Caesar met them in the Campus Martius, and demanded why they had left their encampment without orders and come to the city. They stated in reply, as they had previously planned to do, that they wished to be discharged from the public service. To their great astonishment, Caesar seemed to consider this request as nothing at all extraordinary, but promised, an the other hand, very readily to grant it He said that they should be at once discharged, and should receive faithfully all the rewards which had been promised them at the close of the war for their long and arduous services. At the same time, he expressed his deep regret that, to obtain what he was perfectly willing and ready at any time to grant, they should have so far forgotten their duties as Romans, and violated the discipline which should always be held absolutely sacred by every soldier. He particularly regretted that the tenth legion, on which he had been long accustomed so implicitly to rely, should have taken a part in such transactions.

Its effects.

Attachment of Caesar's soldiers.

In making this address, Caesar assumed a kind and considerate, and even respectful tone toward his men, calling them Quirites instead of soldiers--an honorary mode of appellation, which recognized them as constituent members of the Roman commonwealth. The effect of the whole transaction was what might have been anticipated. A universal desire was awakened throughout the whole army to return to their duty. They sent deputations to Caesar, begging not to be taken at their word, but to be retained in the service, and allowed to accompany him to Africa. After much hesitation and delay, Caesar consented to receive them again, all excepting the tenth legion, who, he said, had now irrevocably lost his confidence and regard. It is a striking illustration of the strength of the attachment which bound Caesar's soldiers to their commander, that the tenth legion would not be discharged, after all. They followed Caesar of their own accord into Africa, earnestly entreating him again and again to receive them. He finally did receive them in detachments, which he incorporated with the rest of his army, or sent on distant service, but he would never organize them as the tenth legion again.

Caesar goes to Africa.

Cato shuts himself up in Africa.

It was now early in the winter, a stormy season for crossing the Mediterranean Sea. Caesar, however, set off from Rome immediately, proceeded south to Sicily, and encamped on the sea-shore there till the fleet was ready to convey his forces to Africa. The usual fortune attended him in the African campaigns His fleet was exposed to imminent dangers in crossing the sea, but, in consequence of the extreme deliberation and skill with which his arrangements were made, he escaped them all. He overcame one after another of the military difficulties which were in his way in Africa. His army endured, in the depth of winter, great exposures and fatigues, and they had to encounter a large hostile force under the charge of Cato. They were, however, successful in every undertaking. Cato retreated at last to the city of Utica, where he shut himself up with the remains of his army; but finding, at length, when Caesar drew near, that there was no hope or possibility of making good his defense, and as his stern and indomitable spirit could not endure the thought of submission to one whom he considered as an enemy to his country and a traitor he resolved upon a very effectual mode of escaping from his conqueror's power.

He stabs himself.

Death of Cato.

He feigned to abandon all hope of defending the city, and began to make arrangements to facilitate the escape of his soldiers over the sea. He collected the vessels in the harbor, and allowed all to embark who were willing to take the risks of the stormy water. He took, apparently, great interest in the embarkations, and, when evening came on, he sent repeatedly down to the sea-side to inquire about the state of the wind and the progress of the operations. At length he retired to his apartment, and, when all was quiet in the house, he lay down upon his bed and stabbed himself with his sword He fell from the bed by the blow, or else from the effect of some convulsive motion which the penetrating steel occasioned. His son and servants, hearing the fall, came rushing into the room, raised him from the floor, and attempted to bind up and stanch the wound. Cato would not permit them to do it. He resisted them violently as soon as he was conscious of what they intended. Finding that a struggle would only aggravate the horrors of the scene, and even hasten its termination, they left the bleeding hero to his fate, and in a few minutes he died.

Folly of his suicide.

The character of Cato, and the circumstances under which his suicide was committed, make it, on the whole, the most conspicuous act of suicide which history records; and the events which followed show in an equally conspicuous manner the extreme folly of the deed. In respect to its wickedness, Cato, not having had the light of Christianity before him, is to be leniently judged. As to the folly of the deed, however, he is to be held strictly accountable. If he had lived and yielded to his conqueror, as he might have done gracefully and without dishonor, since all his means of resistance were exhausted, Caesar would have treated him with generosity and respect, and would have taken him to Rome; and as within a year or two of this time Caesar himself was no more, Cato's vast influence and power might have been, and un doubtedly would have been, called most effectually into action for the benefit of his country. If any one, in defending Cato, should say he could not foresee this, we reply, he could have foreseen it; not the precise events, indeed, which occurred, but he could have foreseen that vast changes must take place, and new aspects of affairs arise, in which his powers would be called into requisition. We can always foresee in the midst of any storm, however dark and gloomy, that clear skies will certainly sooner or later come again; and this is just as true metaphorically in respect to the vicissitudes of human life, as it is literally in regard to the ordinary phenomena of the skies.

Caesar in Spain.

Defeat of Pompey's sons.

From Africa Caesar returned to Rome, and from Rome he went to subdue the resistance which was offered by the sons of Pompey in Spain. He was equally successful here. The oldest son was wounded in battle, and was carried off from the field upon a litter faint and almost dying. He recovered in some degree, and, finding escape from the eager pursuit of Caesar's soldiers impossible, he concealed himself in a cave, where he lingered for a little time in destitution and misery. He was discovered at last; his head was cut off by his captors and sent to Caesar, as his father's had been. The younger son succeeded in escaping, but he became a wretched fugitive and outlaw, and all manifestations of resistance to Caesar's sway disappeared from Spain. The conqueror returned to Rome the undisputed master of the whole Roman world.

The elephants made torch-bearers.

Caesar's triumphs.

The triumphal car breaks down.

Elephant torch-bearers.

Then came his triumphs. Triumphs were great celebrations, by which military heroes in the days of the Roman commonwealth signalized their victories on their return to the city Caesar's triumphs were four, one for each of his four great successful campaigns, viz., in Egypt, in Asia Minor, in Africa, and in Spain. Each was celebrated on a separate day, and there was an interval of several days between them, to magnify their importance, and swell the general interest which they excited among the vast population of the city. On one of these days, the triumphal car in which Caesar rode, which was most magnificently adorned, broke down on the way, and Caesar was nearly thrown out of it by the shock. The immense train of cars, horses, elephants, flags, banners, captives, and trophies which formed the splendid procession was all stopped by the accident, and a considerable delay ensued. Night came on, in fact before the column could again be put in motion to enter the city, and then Caesar, whose genius was never more strikingly shown than when he had opportunity to turn a calamity to advantage, conceived the idea of employing the forty elephants of the train as torch-bearers; the long procession accordingly advanced through the streets and ascended to the Capitol, lighted by the great blazing flambeaus which the sagacious and docile beasts were easily taught to bear, each elephant holding one in his proboscis, and waving it above the crowd around him.

Trophies and emblems.

In these triumphal processions, every thing was borne in exhibition which could serve as a symbol of the conquered country or a trophy of victory, Flags and banners taken from the enemy; vessels of gold and silver, and other treasures, loaded in vans; wretched captives conveyed in open carriages or marching sorrowfully on foot, and destined, some of them, to public execution when the ceremony of the triumph was ended; displays of arms, and implements, and dresses, and all else which might serve to give the Roman crowd an idea of the customs and usages of the remote and conquered nations; the animals they used, caparisoned in the manner in which they used them: these, and a thousand other trophies and emblems, were brought into the line to excite the admiration of the crowd, and to add to the gorgeousness of the spectacle. In fact, it was always a great object of solicitude and exertion with all the Roman generals, when on distant and dangerous expeditions, to possess themselves of every possible prize in the progress of their campaign which could aid in adding splendor to the triumph which was to signalize its end.

Banners and paintings.

In these triumphs of Caesar, a young sister of Cleopatra was in the line of the Egyptian procession. In that devoted to Asia Minor was a great banner containing the words already referred to, Veni, Vidi, Vici. There were great paintings, too, borne aloft, representing battles and other striking scenes. Of course, all Rome was in the highest state of excitement during the days of the exhibition of this pageantry. The whole surrounding country flocked to the capital to witness it, and Caesar's greatness and glory were signalized in the most conspicuous manner to all mankind.

Public entertainments.

Various spectacles and amusements.

Naval combats.

After these triumphs, a series of splendid public entertainments were given, over twenty thousand tables having been spread for the populace of the city Shows of every possible character and variety were exhibited. There were dramatic plays, and equestrian performances in the circus, and gladiatorial combats, and battles with wild beasts, and dances, and chariot races, and every other imaginable amusement which could be devised and carried into effect to gratify a population highly cultivated in all the arts of life, but barbarous and cruel in heart and character. Some of the accounts which have come down to us of the magnificence of the scale on which these entertainments were conducted are absolutely incredible. It is said, for example, that an immense basin was constructed near the Tiber, large enough to contain two fleets of galleys, which had on board two thousand rowers each, and one thousand fighting men. These fleets were then manned with captives, the one with Asiatics and the other with Egyptians, and when all was ready, they were compelled to fight a real battle for the amusement of the spectators which thronged the shores, until vast numbers were killed, and the waters of the lake were dyed with blood. It is also said that the whole Forum, and some of the great streets in the neighborhood where the principal gladiatorial shows were held, were covered with silken awnings to protect the vast crowds of spectators from the sun, and thousands of tents were erected to accommodate the people from the surrounding country, whom the buildings of the city could not contain.

Caesar's power.

Honors conferred upon him.

All open opposition to Caesar's power and dominion now entirely disappeared. Even the Senate vied with the people in rendering him every possible honor. The supreme power had been hitherto lodged in the hands of two consuls, chosen annually, and the Roman people had been extremely jealous of any distinction for any one, higher than that of an elective annual office, with a return to private life again when the brief period should have expired. They now, however, made Caesar, in the first place, consul for ten years, and then Perpetual Dictator. They conferred upon him the title of the Father of his Country. The name of the month in which he was born was changed to Julius, from his praenomen, and we still retain the name. He was made, also, commander-in-chief of all the armies of the commonwealth, the title to which vast military power was expressed in the Latin language by the word IMPERATOR.

Statues of Caesar.

Caesar was highly elated with all these substantial proofs of the greatness and glory to which he had attained, and was also very evidently gratified with smaller, but equally expressive proofs of the general regard. Statues representing his person were placed in the public edifices, and borne in processions like those of the gods. Conspicuous and splendidly ornamented seats were constructed for him in all the places of public assembly, and on these he sat to listen to debates or witness spectacles, as if he were upon a throne He had, either by his influence or by his direct power, the control of all the appointments to office, and was, in fact, in every thing but the name, a sovereign and an absolute king.

His plans of internal improvement.

He began now to form great schemes of internal improvement for the general benefit of the empire. He wished to increase still more the great obligations which the Roman people were under to him for what he had already done. They really were under vast obligations to him; for, considering Rome as a community which was to subsist by governing the world, Caesar had immensely enlarged the means of its subsistence by establishing its sway every where, and providing for an incalculable increase of its revenues from the tribute and the taxation of conquered provinces and kingdoms. Since this work of conquest was now completed, he turned his attention to the internal affairs of the empire, and made many improvements in the system of administration, looking carefully into every thing, and introducing every where those exact and systematic principles which such a mind as his seeks instinctively in every thing over which it has any control.

Ancient division of time.

Change effected by Caesar.

The old and new styles.

One great change which he effected continues in perfect operation throughout Europe to the present day. It related to the division of time. The system of months in use in his day corresponded so imperfectly with the annual circuit of the sun, that the months were moving continually along the year in such a manner that the winter months came at length in the summer, and the summer months in the winter. This led to great practical inconveniences; for whenever, for example, any thing was required by law to be done in certain months, intending to have them done in the summer, and the specified month came at length to be a winter month, the law would require the thing to be done in exactly the wrong season. Caesar remedied all this by adopting a new system of months, which should give three hundred and sixty-five days to the year for three years, and three hundred and sixty-six for the fourth; and so exact was the system which he thus introduced, that it went on unchanged for sixteen centuries. The months were then found to be eleven days out of the way, when a new correction was introduced, and it will now go on three thousand years before the error will amount to a single day. Caesar employed a Greek astronomer to arrange the system that he adopted; and it was in part on account of the improvement which he thus effected that one of the months, as has already been mentioned, was called July. Its name before was Quintilis.

Magnificent schemes.

Caesar collects the means to carry out his vast schemes.

Caesar formed a great many other vast and magnificent schemes. He planned public buildings for the city, which were going to exceed in magnitude and splendor all the edifices of the world. He commenced the collection of vast libraries, formed plans for draining the Pontine Marshes, for bringing great supplies of water into the city by an aqueduct, for cutting a new passage for the Tiber from Rome to the sea, and making an enormous artificial harbor at its mouth. He was going to make a road along the Apennines, and cut a canal through the Isthmus of Corinth, and construct other vast works, which were to make Rome the center of the commerce of the world. In a word, his head was filled with the grandest schemes, and he was gathering around him all the means and resources necessary for the execution of them.

## CHAPTER XI.: THE CONSPIRACY.

Caesar's greatness and glory came at last to a very sudden and violent end. He was assassinated. All the attendant circumstances of this deed, too, were of the most extraordinary character, and thus the dramatic interest which adorns all parts of the great conqueror's history marks strikingly its end.

Jealousies awakened by Caesar's power.

The Roman Constitution.

Struggles and Conflicts.

His prosperity and power awakened, of course, a secret jealousy and ill will. Those who were disappointed in their expectations of his favor murmured. Others, who had once been his rivals, hated him for having triumphed over them. Then there was a stern spirit of democracy, too, among certain classes of the citizens of Rome which could not brook a master. It is true that the sovereign power in the Roman commonwealth had never been shared by all the inhabitants. It was only in certain privileged classes that the sovereignty was vested; but among these the functions of government were divided and distributed in such a way as to balance one interest against another, and to give all their proper share of influence and authority. Terrible struggles and conflicts often occurred among these various sections of society, as one or another attempted from time to time to encroach upon the rights or privileges of the rest. These struggles, however, ended usually in at last restoring again the equilibrium which had been disturbed. No one power could ever gain the entire ascendency; and thus, as all monarchism seemed excluded from their system, they called it a republic. Caesar, however, had now concentrated in himself all the principal elements of power, and there began to be suspicions that he wished to make himself in name and openly, as well as secretly and in fact, a king.

Roman repugnance to royalty.

Firmness of the Romans.

The Romans abhorred the very name of king. They had had kings in the early periods of their history, but they made themselves odious by their pride and their oppressions, and the people had deposed and expelled them. The modern nations of Europe have several times performed the same exploit, but they have generally felt unprotected and ill at ease without a personal sovereign over them and have accordingly, in most cases, after a few years, restored some branch of the expelled dynasty to the throne The Romans were more persevering and firm. They had managed their empire now for five hundred years as a republic, and though they had had internal dissensions, conflicts, and quarrels without end, had persisted so firmly and unanimously in their detestation of all regal authority, that no one of the long line of ambitious and powerful statesmen, generals, or conquerors by which the history of the empire had been signalized, had ever dared to aspire to the name of king.

Caesar's ambitious plans.

There began, however, soon to appear some indications that Caesar, who certainly now possessed regal power, would like the regal name. Ambitious men, in such cases, do not directly assume themselves the titles and symbols of royalty. Others make the claim for them, while they faintly disavow it, till they have opportunity to gee what effect the idea produces on the public mind. The following incidents occurred which it was thought indicated such a design on the part of Caesar.

American feeling.

There were in some of the public buildings certain statues of kings; for it must be understood that the Roman dislike to kings was only a dislike to having kingly authority exercised over themselves. They respected and sometimes admired the kings of other countries, and honored their exploits, and made statues to commemorate their fame. They were willing that kings should reign elsewhere, so long as there were no king of Rome. The American feeling at the present day is much the same. If the Queen of England were to make a progress through this country, she would receive, perhaps, as many and as striking marks of attention and honor as would be rendered to her in her own realm. We venerate the antiquity of her royal line; we admire the efficiency of her government and the sublime grandeur of her empire, and have as high an idea as any, of the powers and prerogatives of her crown--and these feelings would show themselves most abundantly on any proper occasion. We are willing, nay, wish that she should continue to reign over Englishmen; and yet, after all, it would take some millions of bayonets to place a queen securely upon a throne over this land.

Regal power.

Regal power was accordingly, in the abstract, looked up to at Rome, as it is elsewhere, with great respect; and it was, in fact, all the more tempting as an object of ambition, from the determination felt by the people that it should not be exercised there. There were, accordingly, statues of kings at Rome. Caesar placed his own statue among them. Some approved, others murmured.

Caesar's seat in the theater.

There was a public theater in the city, where the officers of the government were accustomed to sit in honorable seats prepared expressly for them, those of the Senate being higher and more distinguished than the rest. Caesar had a seat prepared for himself there, similar in form to a throne, and adorned it magnificently with gilding and ornaments of gold, which gave it the entire pre-eminence over all the other seats.

He had a similar throne placed in the senate chamber, to be occupied by himself when attending there, like the throne of the King of England in the House of Lords.

Public celebrations.

Caesar receives the Senate sitting.

Consequent excitement.

He held, moreover, a great many public celebrations and triumphs in the city in commemoration of his exploits and honors; and, on one of these occasions, it was arranged that the Senate were to come to him at a temple in a body, and announce to him certain decrees which they had passed to his honor. Vast crowds had assembled to witness the ceremony Caesar was seated in a magnificent chair, which might have been called either a chair or a throne, and was surrounded by officers and attendants When the Senate approached, Caesar did not rise to receive them, but remained seated, like a monarch receiving a deputation of his subjects. The incident would not seem to be in itself of any great importance, but, considered as an indication of Caesar's designs, it attracted great attention, and produced a very general excitement. The act was adroitly managed so as to be somewhat equivocal in its character, in order that it might be represented one way or the other on the following day, according as the indications of public sentiment might incline. Some said that Caesar was intending to rise, but was prevented, and held down by those who stood around him. Others said that an officer motioned to him to rise, but he rebuked his interference by a frown, and continued his seat. Thus while, in fact, he received the Roman Senate as their monarch and sovereign, his own intentions and designs in so doing were left somewhat in doubt, in order to avoid awakening a sudden and violent opposition.

Caesar's statute crowned.

Not long after this, as he was returning in public from some great festival, the streets being full of crowds, and the populace following him in great throngs with loud acclamations, a man went up to his statue as he passed it, and placed upon the head of it a laurel crown, fastened with a white ribbon, which was a badge of royalty. Some officers ordered the ribbon to be taken down, and sent the man to prison. Caesar was very much displeased with the officers, and dismissed them from their office. He wished, he said, to have the opportunity to disavow, himself, such claims, and not to have others disavow them for him.

Caesar's disavowals.

Caesar's disavowals were, however, so faint, and people had so little confidence in their sincerity, that the cases became more and more frequent in which the titles and symbols of royalty were connected with his name. The people who wished to gain his favor saluted him in public with the name of Rex, the Latin word for king. He replied that his name was Caesar, not Rex, showing, however, no other signs of displeasure. On one great occasion, a high public officer, a near relative of his, repeatedly placed a diadem upon his head, Caesar himself, as often as he did it, gently putting it off. At last he sent the diadem away to a temple that was near, saying that there was no king in Rome but Jupiter. In a word, all his conduct indicated that he wished to have it appear that the people were pressing the crown upon him, when he himself was steadily refusing it.

Some willing to make Caesar king.

Others oppose it.

This state of things produced a very strong and universal, though suppressed excitement in the city. Parties were formed. Some began to be willing to make Caesar king; others were determined to hazard their lives to prevent it. None dared, however, openly to utter their sentiments on either side. They expressed them by mysterious looks and dark intimations. At the time when Caesar refused to rise to receive the Senate, many of the members withdrew in silence, and with looks of offended dignity When the crown was placed upon his statue or upon his own brow, a portion of the populace would applaud with loud acclamations; and whenever he disavowed these acts, either by words or counter-actions of his own, an equally loud acclamation would arise from the other side. On the whole, however, the idea that Caesar was gradually advancing toward the kingdom steadily gained ground.

Caesar's pretexts.

His assumed humility.

And yet Caesar himself spoke frequently with great humility in respect to his pretensions and claims; and when he found public sentiment turning against the ambitious schemes he seems secretly to have cherished, he would present some excuse or explanation for his conduct plausible enough to answer the purpose of a disavowal. When he received the Senate, sitting like a king, on the occasion before referred to, when they read to him the decrees which they had passed in his favor, he replied to them that there was more need of diminishing the public honors which he received than of increasing them. When he found, too, how much excitement his conduct on that occasion had produced, he explained it by saying that he had retained his sitting posture on account of the infirmity of his health, as it made him dizzy to stand. He thought, probably, that these pretexts would tend to quiet the strong and turbulent spirits around him, from whose envy or rivalry he had most to fear, without at all interfering with the effect which the act itself would have produced upon the masses of the population. He wished, in a word, to accustom them to see him assume the position and the bearing of a sovereign, while, by his apparent humility in his intercourse with those immediately around him, he avoided as much as possible irritating and arousing the jealous and watchful rivals who were next to him in power.

Progress of Caesar's plans.

If this were his plan, it seemed to be advancing prosperously toward its accomplishment. The population of the city seemed to become more and more familiar with the idea that Caesar was about to become a king. The opposition which the idea had at first awakened appeared to subside, or, at least, the public expression of it, which daily became more and more determined and dangerous, was restrained. At length the time arrived when it appeared safe to introduce the subject to the Roman Senate. This, of course, was a hazardous experiment. It was managed, however, in a very adroit and ingenious manner.

The Sibylline books.

Declaration of the Sibylline books.

Plan for crowning Caesar.

There were in Rome, and, in fact, in many other cities and countries of the world in those days, a variety of prophetic books, called the Sibylline Oracles, in which it was generally believed that future events were foretold. Some of these volumes or rolls, which were very ancient and of great authority, were preserved in the temples at Rome, under the charge of a board of guardians, who were to keep them with the utmost care, and to consult them on great occasions, in order to discover beforehand what would be the result of public measures or great enterprises which were in contemplation. It happened that at this time the Romans were engaged in a war with the Parthians, a very wealthy and powerful nation of Asia. Caesar was making preparations for an expedition to the East to attempt to subdue this people. He gave orders that the Sibylline Oracles should be consulted. The proper officers, after consulting them with the usual solemn ceremonies, reported to the Senate that they found it recorded in these sacred prophecies that the Parthians could not be conquered except by a king, A senator proposed, therefore, that, to meet the emergency, Caesar should be made king during the war. There was at first no decisive action on this proposal. It was dangerous to express any opinion. People were thoughtful, serious, and silent, as on the eve of some great convulsion. No one knew what others were meditating, and thus did not dare to express his own wishes or designs. There soon, however, was a prevailing understanding that Caesar's friends were determined on executing the design of crowning him, and that the fifteenth of March, called, in their phraseology, the Ides of March, was fixed upon as the coronation day.

The conspiracy.

In the mean time, Caesar's enemies, though to all outward appearance quiet and calm, had not been inactive. Finding that his plans were now ripe for execution, and that they had no, open means of resisting them, they formed a conspiracy to assassinate Caesar himself, and thus bring his ambitious schemes to an effectual and final end. The name of the original leader of this conspiracy was Cassius.

Cassius.

Cassius had been for a long time Caesar's personal rival and enemy. He was a man of a very violent and ardent temperament, impetuous and fearless, very fond of exercising power himself, but very restless and uneasy in having it exercised over him. He had all the Roman repugnance to being under the authority of a master, with an additional personal determination of his own not to submit to Caesar. He determined to slay Caesar rather than to allow him to be made a king, and he went to work, with great caution, to bring other leading and influential men to join him in this determination. Some of those to whom he applied said that they would unite with him in his plot provided he would get Marcus Brutus to join them.

Marcus Brutus.

Brutus was the praetor of the city. The praetorship of the city was a very high municipal office. The conspirators wished to have Brutus join them partly on account of his station as a magistrate, as if they supposed that by having the highest public magistrate of the city for their leader in the deed, the destruction of their victim would appear less like a murder, and would be invested, instead, in some respects, with the sanctions and with the dignity of an official execution.

Character of Brutus.

His firmness and courage.

Then, again, they wished for the moral support which would be afforded them in their desperate enterprise by Brutus's extraordinary personal character. He was younger than Cassius, but he was grave, thoughtful, taciturn, calm--a man of inflexible integrity, of the coolest determination, and, at the same time, of the most undaunted courage. The conspirators distrusted one another, for the resolution of impetuous men is very apt to fail when the emergency arrives which puts it to the test; but as for Brutus, they knew very well that whatever he undertook he would most certainly do.

The ancient Brutus.

His expulsion of the kings.

There was a great deal even in his name. It was a Brutus that five centuries before had been the main instrument of the expulsion of the Roman kings. He had secretly meditated the design, and, the better to conceal it, had feigned idiocy, as the story was, that he might not be watched or suspected until the favorable hour for executing his design should arrive. He therefore ceased to speak, and seemed to lose his reason; he wandered about the city silent and gloomy, like a brute. His name had been Lucius Junius before. They added Brutus now, to designate his condition. When at last, however, the crisis arrived which he judged favorable for the expulsion of the kings, he suddenly reassumed his speech and his reason, called the astonished Romans to arms, and triumphantly accomplished his design. His name and memory had been cherished ever since that day as of a great deliverer.

The history of Brutus.

They, therefore, who looked upon Caesar as another king, naturally turned their thoughts to the Brutus of their day, hoping to find in him another deliverer. Brutus found, from time to time, inscriptions on his ancient namesake's statue expressing the wish that he were now alive. He also found each morning, as he came to the tribunal where he was accustomed to sit in the discharge of the duties of his office, brief writings, which had been left there during the night, in which few words expressed deep meaning, such as "Awake, Brutus, to thy duty;" and "Art thou indeed a Brutus?"

His obligations to Caesar.

Caesar's friendship for Brutus.

Still it seemed hardly probable that Brutus could be led to take a decided stand against Caesar, for they had been warm personal friends ever since the conclusion of the civil wars. Brutus had, indeed, been on Pompey's side while that general lived; he fought with him at the battle of Pharsalia, but he had been taken prisoner there, and Caesar, instead of executing him as a traitor, as most victorious generals in a civil war would have done, spared his life, forgave him for his hostility, received him into his own service, and afterward raised him to very high and honorable stations. He gave him the government of the richest province, and, after his return from it, loaded with wealth and honors, he made him praetor of the city. In a word, it would seem that he had done every thing which it was possible to do to make him one of his most trustworthy and devoted friends. The men, therefore, to whom Cassius first applied, perhaps thought that they were very safe in saying that they would unite in the intended conspiracy if he would get Brutus to join them. They expected Cassius himself to make the attempt to secure the co-operation of Brutus, as Cassius was on terms of intimacy with him on account of a family connection. Cassius's wife was the sister of Brutus. This had made the two men intimate associates and warm friends in former years, though they had been recently somewhat estranged from each other on account of having been competitors for the same offices and honors. In these contests Caesar had decided in favor of Brutus. "Cassius," said he, on one such occasion, "gives the best reasons; but I can not refuse Brutus any thing he asks for." In fact, Caesar had conceived a strong personal friendship for Brutus, and believed him to be entirely devoted to his cause.

Interview between Brutus and Cassius.

Cassius, however, sought an interview with Brutus, with a view of engaging him in his design. He easily effected his own reconciliation with him, as he had himself been the offended party in their estrangement from each other. He asked Brutus whether he intended to be present in the Senate on the Ides of March, when the friends of Caesar, as was understood, were intending to present him with the crown. Brutus said he should not be there. "But suppose," said Cassius, "we are specially summoned." "Then," said Brutus, "I shall go, and shall be ready to die if necessary to defend the liberty of my country."

Arguments of Cassius.

Cassius then assured Brutus that there were many other Roman citizens, of the highest rank, who were animated by the same determination, and that they all looked up to him to lead and direct them in the work which it was now very evident must be done. "Men look," said Cassius, "to other praetors to entertain them with games, spectacles, and shows, but they have very different ideas in respect to you. Your character, your name, your position, your ancestry, and the course of conduct which you have already always pursued, inspire the whole city with the hope that you are to be their deliverer. The citizens are all ready to aid you, and to sustain you at the hazard of their lives; but they look to you to go forward, and to act in their name and in their behalf, in the crisis which is now approaching."

Effect on Brutus.

Brutus engages in the conspiracy.

Men of a very calm exterior are often susceptible of the profoundest agitations within, the emotions seeming to be sometimes all the more permanent and uncontrollable from the absence of outward display. Brutus said little, but his soul was excited and fired by Cassius's words. There was a struggle in his soul between his grateful sense of his political obligations to Caesar and his personal attachment to him on the one hand, and, on the other, a certain stern Roman conviction that every thing should be sacrificed, even friendship and gratitude, as well as fortune and life, to the welfare of his country. He acceded to the plan, and began forthwith to enter upon the necessary measures for putting it into execution.

Ligurius.

There was a certain general, named Ligurius, who had been in Pompey's army, and whose hostility to Caesar had never been really subdued. He was now sick. Brutus went to see him. He found him in his bed. The excitement in Rome was so intense, though the expressions of it were suppressed and restrained, that every one was expecting continually some great event, and every motion and look was interpreted to have some deep meaning. Ligurius read in the countenance of Brutus, as he approached his bedside, that he had not come on any trifling errand. "Ligurius," said Brutus, "this is not a time for you to be sick." "Brutus," replied Ligurius, rising at once from his couch, "if you have any enterprise in mind that is worthy of you, I am well." Brutus explained to the sick man their design, and he entered into it with ardor.

Consultations of the conspirators.

Their bold plan.

Final arrangements.

The plan was divulged to one after another of such men as the conspirators supposed most worthy of confidence in such a desperate undertaking, and meetings for consultation were held to determine what plan to adopt for finally accomplishing their end. It was agreed that Caesar must be slain; but the time, the place, and the manner in which the deed should be performed were all yet undecided. Various plans were proposed in the consultations which the conspirators held; but there was one thing peculiar to them all, which was, that they did not any of them contemplate or provide for any thing like secrecy in the commission of the deed. It was to be performed in the most open and public manner. With a stern and undaunted boldness, which has always been considered by mankind as truly sublime, they determined that, in respect to the actual execution itself of the solemn judgment which they had pronounced, there should be nothing private or concealed. They thought over the various public situations in which they might find Caesar, and where they might strike him down, only to select the one which would be most public of all. They kept, of course, their preliminary counsels private, to prevent the adoption of measures for counteracting them; but they were to perform the deed in such a manner as that, so soon as it was performed, they should stand out to view, exposed fully to the gaze of all mankind as the authors, of it. They planned no retreat, no concealment, no protection whatever for themselves, seeming to feel that the deed which they were about to perform, of destroying the master and monarch of the world, was a deed in its own nature so grand and sublime as to raise the perpetrators of it entirely above all considerations relating to their own personal safety. Their plan, therefore, was to keep their consultations and arrangements secret until they were prepared to strike the blow, then to strike it in the most public and imposing manner possible, and calmly afterward to await the consequences.

The place and the day.

In this view of the subject, they decided that the chamber of the Roman Senate was the proper place, and the Ides of March, the day on which he was appointed to be crowned, was the propel time for Caesar to be slain.

## CHAPTER XII.: THE ASSASSINATION.

Caesar receives many warnings of his approaching fate.

According to the account given by his historians, Caesar received many warnings of his approaching fate, which, however, he would not heed. Many of these warnings were strange portents and prodigies, which the philosophical writers who recorded them half believed themselves, and which they were always ready to add to their narratives even if they did not believe them, on account of the great influence which such an introduction of the supernatural and the divine had with readers in those days in enhancing the dignity and the dramatic interest of the story. These warnings were as follows:

The tomb and inscription.

At Capua, which was a great city at some distance south of Rome, the second, in fact, in Italy, and the one which Hannibal had proposed to make his capital, some workmen were removing certain ancient sepulchers to make room for the foundations of a splendid edifice which, among his other plans for the embellishment of the cities of Italy, Caesar was intending to have erected there. As the excavations advanced, the workmen came at last to an ancient tomb, which proved to be that of the original founder of Capua; and, in bringing out the sarcophagus, they found an inscription, worked upon a brass plate, and in the Greek character, predicting that if those remains were ever disturbed, a great member of the Julian family would be assassinated by his own friends, and his death would be followed by extended devastations throughout all Italy.

Caesar's horses.

The horses, too, with which Caesar had passed the Rubicon, and which had been, ever since that time, living in honorable retirement in a splendid park which Caesar had provided for them, by some mysterious instinct, or from some divine communication, had warning of the approach of their great benefactor's end. They refused their food, and walked about with melancholy and dejected looks, mourning apparently, and in a manner almost human, some impending grief.

The soothsayers.

There was a class of prophets in those days called by a name which has been translated soothsayers. These soothsayers were able, as was supposed, to look somewhat into futurity-- dimly and doubtfully, it is true, but really, by means of certain appearances exhibited by the bodies of the animals offered in sacrifices These soothsayers were consulted on all important occasions; and if the auspices proved unfavorable when any great enterprise was about to be undertaken, it was often, on that account, abandoned or postponed. One of these soothsayers, named Spurinna, came to Caesar one day, and informed him that he had found, by means of a public sacrifice which he had just been offering, that there was a great and mysterious danger impending over him, which was connected in some way with the Ides of March, and he counseled him to be particularly cautious and circumspect until that day should have passed.

The hawks and the wren.

The Senate were to meet on the Ides of March in a new and splendid edifice, which had been erected for their use by Pompey. There was in the interior of the building, among other decorations, a statue of Pompey. The day before the Ides of March, some birds of prey from a neighboring grove came flying into this hall, pursuing a little wren with a sprig of laurel in its mouth. The birds tore the wren to pieces, the laurel dropping from its bill to the marble pavement of the floor below. Now, as Caesar had been always accustomed to wear a crown of laurel on great occasions, and had always evinced a particular fondness for that decoration, that plant had come to be considered his own proper badge, and the fall of the laurel, therefore, was naturally thought to portend some great calamity to him.

Caesar's agitation of mind.

His dream.

Calpurnia's dream.

The effect of a disturbed mind.

The night before the Ides of March Caesar could not sleep. It would not seem, however, to be necessary to suppose any thing supernatural to account for his wakefulness. He lay upon his bed restless and excited, or if he fell into a momentary slumber, his thoughts, instead of finding repose, were only plunged into greater agitations, produced by strange, and, as he thought, supernatural dreams. He imagined that he ascended into the skies, and was received there by Jupiter, the supreme divinity, as an associate and equal. While shaking hands with the great father of gods and men, the sleeper was startled by a frightful sound. He awoke, and found his wife Calpurnia groaning and struggling in her sleep. He saw her by the moonlight which was shining into the room. He spoke to her, and aroused her. After staring wildly for a moment till she had recovered her thoughts, she said that she had had a dreadful dream. She had dreamed that the roof of the house had fallen in, and that, at the same instant, the doors had been burst open, and some robber or assassin had stabbed her husband as he was lying in her arms. The philosophy of those days found in these dreams mysterious and preternatural warnings of impending danger; that of ours, however, sees nothing either in the absurd sacrilegiousness of Caesar's thoughts, or his wife's incoherent and inconsistent images of terror--nothing more than the natural and proper effects, on the one hand, of the insatiable ambition of man, and, on the other, of the conjugal affection and solicitude of woman. The ancient sculptors carved out images of men, by the forms and lineaments of which we see that the physical characteristics of humanity have not changed. History seems to do the same with the affections and passions of the soul. The dreams of Caesar and his wife on the night before the Ides of March, as thus recorded, form a sort of spiritual statue, which remains from generation to generation, to show us how precisely all the inward workings of human nature are from age to age the same.

Caesar hesitates.

When the morning came Caesar and Calpurnia arose, both restless and ill at ease. Caesar ordered the auspices to be consulted with reference to the intended proceedings of the day. The soothsayers came in in due time, and reported that the result was unfavorable. Calpurnia, too, earnestly entreated her husband not to go to the senate-house that day. She had a very strong presentiment that, if he did go, some great calamity would ensue. Caesar himself hesitated. He was half inclined to yield, and postpone his coronation to another occasion.

Decimus Brutus.

In the course of the day, while Caesar was in this state of doubt and uncertainty, one of the conspirators, named Decimus Brutus, came in. This Brutus was not a man of any extraordinary courage or energy, but he had been invited by the other conspirators to join them, on account of his having under his charge a large number of gladiators, who, being desperate and reckless men, would constitute a very suitable armed force for them to call in to their aid in case of any emergency arising which should require it.

Decimus Brutus waits upon Caesar.

The conspirators having thus all their plans arranged, Decimus Brutus was commissioned to call at Caesar's house when the time approached for the assembling of the Senate, both to avert suspicion from Caesar's mind, and to assure himself that nothing had been discovered It was in the afternoon, the time for the meeting of the senators having been fixed at five o'clock. Decimus Brutus found Caesar troubled and perplexed, and uncertain what to do. After hearing what he had to say, he replied by urging him to go by all means to the senate-house, as he had intended. "You have formally called the Senate together," said he, "and they are now assembling. They are all prepared to confer upon you the rank and title of king, not only in Parthia, while you are conducting this war but every where, by sea and land, except in Italy. And now, while they are all in their places, waiting to consummate the great act, how absurd will it be for you to send them word to go home again, and come back some other day, when Calpurnia shall have had better dreams!"

He persuades him to go.

He urged, too, that, even if Caesar was determined to put off the action of the Senate to another day, he was imperiously bound to go himself and adjourn the session in person. So saying, he took the hesitating potentate by the arm, and adding to his arguments a little gentle force, conducted him along.

Artemidorus discovers the plot.

He warns Caesar.

The conspirators supposed that all was safe The fact was, however, that all had been discovered. There was a certain Greek, a teacher of oratory, named Artemidorus. He had contrived to learn something of the plot from some of the conspirators who were his pupils. He wrote a brief statement of the leading particulars, and, having no other mode of access to Caesar, he determined to hand it to him on the way as he went to the senate-house. Of course, the occasion was one of great public interest, and crowds had assembled in the streets to see the great conqueror as he went along. As usual at such times, when powerful officers of state appear in public, many people came up to present petitions to him as he passed. These he received, and handed them, without reading, to his secretary who attended him, as if to have them preserved for future examination. Artemidorus, who was waiting for his opportunity, when he perceived what disposition Caesar made of the papers which were given to him, began to be afraid that his own communication would not be attended to until it was too late. He accordingly pressed up near to Caesar, refusing to allow any one else to pass the paper in; and when, at last, he obtained an opportunity, he gave it directly into Caesar's hands saying to him, "Read this immediately: it concerns yourself, and is of the utmost importance"

Caesar took the paper and attempted to read it, but new petitions and other interruptions constantly prevented him; finally he gave up the attempt, and went on his way, receiving and passing to his secretary all other papers, but retaining this paper of Artemidorus in his hand.

Caesar and Spurinna.

Caesar passed Spurinna on his way to the senate-house--the soothsayer who had predicted some great danger connected with the Ides of March. As soon as he recognized him, he accosted him with the words, "Well, Spurinna, the Ides of March have come, and I am safe." "Yes," replied Spurinna, "they have come, but they are not yet over."

Caesar arrives at the senate house.

At length he arrived at the senate-house, with the paper of Artemidorus still unread in his hand. The senators were all convened, the leading conspirators among them. They all rose to receive Caesar as he entered. Caesar advanced to the seat provided for him, and, when he was seated, the senators themselves sat down. The moment had now arrived, and the conspirators, with pale looks and beating hearts, felt that now or never the deed was to be done.

Resolution of the Conspirators.

It requires a very considerable degree of physical courage and hardihood for men to come to a calm and deliberate decision that they will kill one whom they hate, and, still more, actually to strike the blow, even when under the immediate impulse of passion. But men who are perfectly capable of either of these often find their resolution fail them as the time comes for striking a dagger into the living flesh of their victim, when he sits at ease and unconcerned before them, unarmed and defenseless, and doing nothing to excite those feelings of irritation and anger which are generally found so necessary to nerve the human arm to such deeds. Utter defenselessness is accordingly, sometimes, a greater protection than an armor of steel.

Caesar and Pompey's statue.

Even Cassius himself, the originator and the soul of the whole enterprise, found his courage hardly adequate to the work now that the moment had arrived; and, in order to arouse the necessary excitement in his soul, he looked up to the statue of Pompey, Caesar's ancient and most formidable enemy, and invoked its aid. It gave him its aid. It inspired him with some portion of the enmity with which the soul of its great original had burned; and thus the soul of the living assassin was nerved to its work by a sort of sympathy with a block of stone.

Plan of the conspirators.

Foreseeing the necessity of something like a stimulus to action when the immediate moment for action should arrive, the conspirators had agreed that, as soon as Caesar was seated, they would approach him with a petition, which he would probably refuse, and then, gathering around him, they would urge him with their importunities, so as to produce, in the confusion, a sort of excitement that would make it easier for them to strike the blow.

Marc Antony.

There was one person, a relative and friend of Caesar's, named Marcus Antonius, called commonly, however, in English narratives, Marc Antony, the same who has been already mentioned as having been subsequently connected with Cleopatra. He was a very energetic and determined man, who, they thought, might possibly attempt to defend him. To prevent this, one of the conspirators had been designated to take him aside, and occupy his attention with some pretended subject of discourse, ready, at the same time, to resist and prevent his interference if he should show himself inclined to offer any.

The petition.

Caesar assaulted.

Things being thus arranged, the petitioner, as had been agreed, advanced to Caesar with his petition, others coming up at the same time as if to second the request. The object of the petition was to ask for the pardon of the brother of one of the conspirators. Caesar declined granting it. The others then crowded around him, urging him to grant the request with pressing importunities, all apparently reluctant to strike the first blow. Caesar began to be alarmed, and attempted to repel them. One of them then pulled down his robe from his neck to lay it bare. Caesar arose, exclaiming, "But this is violence." At the same instant, one of the conspirators struck at him with his sword, and wounded him slightly in the neck.

He resists.

All was now terror, outcry, and confusion Caesar had no time to draw his sword, but fought a moment with his style, a sharp instrument of iron with which they wrote, in those days, on waxen tablets, and which he happened then to have in his hand. With this instrument he ran one of his enemies through the arm.

POMPEY'S STATUE.

Caesar is overcome.

Pompey's statue.

Caesar's death.

This resistance was just what was necessary to excite the conspirators, and give them the requisite resolution to finish their work. Caesar soon saw the swords, accordingly, gleaming all around him, and thrusting themselves at him on every side. The senators rose in confusion and dismay, perfectly thunderstruck at the scene, and not knowing what to do. Antony perceived that all resistance on his part would be unavailing, and accordingly did not attempt any. Caesar defended himself alone for a few minutes as well as he could, looking all around him in vain for help, and retreating at the same time toward the pedestal of Pompey's statue. At length, when he saw Brutus among his murderers, he exclaimed, "And you too, Brutus?" and seemed from that moment to give up in despair. He drew his robe over his face, and soon fell under the wounds which he received. His blood ran out upon the pavement at the foot of Pompey's statue, as if his death were a sacrifice offered to appease his ancient enemy's revenge.

Flight of the senators.

Great commotion.

In the midst of the scene Brutus made an attempt to address the senators, and to vindicate what they had done, but the confusion and excitement were so great that it was impossible that any thing could be heard. The senators were, in fact, rapidly leaving the place, going off in every direction, and spreading the tidings over the city. The event, of course, produced universal commotion. The citizens began to close their shops, and some to barricade their houses, while others hurried to and fro about the streets, anxiously inquiring for intelligence, and wondering what dreadful event was next to be expected. Antony and Lepidus, who were Caesar's two most faithful and influential friends, not knowing how extensive the conspiracy might be, nor how far the hostility to Caesar and his party might extend, fled, and, not daring to go to their own houses, lest the assassins or their confederates might pursue them there, sought concealment in the houses of friends on whom they supposed they could rely and who were willing to receive them.

The Conspirators proceed to the Capitol.

They glory in their deed.

In the mean time, the conspirators, glorying In the deed which they had perpetrated, and congratulating each other on the successful issue of their enterprise, sallied forth together from the senate-house, leaving the body of their victim weltering in its blood, and marched, with drawn swords in their hands, along the streets from the senate-house to the Capitol. Brutus went at the head of them, preceded by a liberty cap borne upon the point of a spear, and with his bloody dagger in his hand. The Capitol was the citadel, built magnificently upon the Capitoline Hill, and surrounded by temples, and other sacred and civil edifices, which made the spot the architectural wonder of the world. As Brutus and his company proceeded thither, they announced to the citizens, as they went along, the great deed of deliverance which they had wrought out for the country. Instead of seeking concealment, they gloried in the work which they had done, and they so far succeeded in inspiring others with a portion of their enthusiasm, that some men who had really taken no part in the deed joined Brutus and his company in their march, to obtain by stealth a share in the glory.

Number of Caesar's wounds.

The body of Caesar lay for some time unheeded where it had fallen, the attention of every one being turned to the excitement, which was extending through the city, and to the expectation of other great events which might suddenly develop themselves in other quarters of Rome. There were left only three of Caesar's slaves, who gathered around the body to look at the wounds. They counted them, and found the number twenty-three. It shows, however, how strikingly, and with what reluctance, the actors in this tragedy came up to their work at last, that of all these twenty-three wounds only one was a mortal one. In fact, it is probable that, while all of the conspirators struck the victim in their turn, to fulfill the pledge which they had given to one another that they would every one inflict a wound, each one hoped that the fatal blow would be given, after all, by some other hand than his own.

His slaves convey his body home.

At last the slaves decided to convey the body home. They obtained a sort of chair, which was made to be borne by poles, and placed the body upon it. Then, lifting at the three handles, and allowing the fourth to hang unsupported for want of a man, they bore the ghastly remains home to the distracted Calpurnia.

Address of the conspirators.

The next day Brutus and his associates called an assembly of the people in the Forum, and made an address to them, explaining the motives which had led them to the commission of the deed, and vindicating the necessity and the justice of it. The people received these explanations in silence. They expressed neither approbation nor displeasure. It was not, in fact, to be expected that they would feel or evince any satisfaction at the loss of their master. He had been their champion, and, as they believed, their friend. The removal of Caesar brought no accession of power nor increase of liberty to them. It might have been a gain to ambitious senators, or powerful generals, or high officers of state, by removing a successful rival out of their way, but it seemed to promise little advantage to the community at large, other than the changing of one despotism for another. Besides, a populace who know that they mast be governed, prefer generally, if they must submit to some control, to yield their submission to some one master spirit whom they can look up to as a great and acknowledged superior. They had rather have a Caesar than a Senate to command them.

Feelings of the populace.

The higher authorities, however, were, at might have been expected, disposed to acquiesce in the removal of Caesar from his intended throne. The Senate met, and passed an act of indemnity, to shield the conspirators from all legal liability for the deed they had done. In order, however, to satisfy the people too, as far as possible, they decreed divine honors to Caesar, confirmed and ratified all that he had done while in the exercise of supreme power, and appointed a time for the funeral, ordering arrangements to be made for a very pompous celebration of it.

Caesar's will.

Its provisions.

A will was soon found, which Caesar, it seems, had made some time before. Calpurnia's father proposed that this will should be opened and read in public at Antony's house; and this was accordingly done. The provisions of the will were, many of them, of such a character as renewed the feelings of interest and sympathy which the people of Rome had begun to cherish for Caesar's memory. His vast estate was divided chiefly among the children of his sister, as he had no children of his own, while the very men who had been most prominent in his assassination were named as trustees and guardians of the property; and one of them, Decimus Brutus, the one who had been so urgent to conduct him to the senate-house, was a second heir. He had some splendid gardens near the Tiber, which he bequeathed to the citizens of Rome, and a large amount of money also, to be divided among them, sufficient to give every man a considerable sum.

Preparations for Caesar's funeral.

The Field of Mars.

The time for the celebration of the funeral ceremonies was made known by proclamation, and, as the concourse of strangers and citizens of Rome was likely to be so great as to forbid the forming of all into one procession without consuming more than one day, the various classes of the community were invited to come, each in their own way, to the Field of Mars, bringing with them such insignia, offerings, and oblations as they pleased. The Field of Mars was an immense parade ground, reserved for military reviews, spectacles, and shows. A funeral pile was erected here for the burning of the body There was to be a funeral discourse pronounced, and Marc Antony had been designated to perform this duty. The body had been placed in a gilded bed, under a magnificent canopy in the form of a temple, before the rostra where the funeral discourse was to be pronounced. The bed was covered with scarlet and cloth of gold and at the head of it was laid the robe in which Caesar had been slain. It was stained with blood, and pierced with the holes that the swords and daggers of the conspirators had made.

Marc Antony's oration.

The funeral pile.

Marc Antony, instead of pronouncing a formal panegyric upon his deceased friend, ordered a crier to read the decrees of the Senate, in which all honors, human and divine, had been ascribed to Caesar. He then added a few words of his own. The bed was then taken up, with the body upon it, and borne out into the Forum, preparatory to conveying it to the pile which had been prepared for it upon the Field of Mars, A question, however, here arose among the multitude assembled in respect to the proper place for burning the body. The people seemed inclined to select the most honorable place which could be found within the limits of the city. Some proposed a beautiful temple on the Capitoline Hill. Others wished to take it to the senate-house, where he had been slain. The Senate, and those who were less inclined to pay extravagant honors to the departed hero, were in favor of some more retired spot, under pretense that the buildings of the city would be endangered by the fire. This discussion was fast becoming a dispute, when it was suddenly ended by two men, with swords at their sides and knees in their hands, forcing their way through the crowd with lighted torches, and setting the bed and its canopy on fire where it lay.

BURNING OF CAESAR'S BODY.

The body burned in the Forum.

This settled the question, and the whole company were soon in the wildest excitement with the work of building up a funeral pile upon the spot. At first they brought fagots and threw upon the fire, then benches from the neighboring courts and porticoes, and then any thing combustible which came to hand. The honor done to the memory of a deceased hero was, in some sense, in proportion to the greatness of his funeral pile, and all the populace on this occasion began soon to seize every thing they could find, appropriate and unappropriate, provided that it would increase the flame. The soldiers threw on their lances and spears, the musicians their instruments, and others stripped off the cloths and trappings from the furniture of the procession, and heaped them upon the burning pile.

The conflagration.

So fierce and extensive was the fire, that it spread to some of the neighboring houses, and required great efforts to prevent a general conflagration. The people, too, became greatly excited by the scene. They lighted torches by the fire, and went to the houses of Brutus and Cassius, threatening vengeance upon them for the murder of Caesar. The authorities succeeded though with infinite difficulty, in protecting Brutus and Cassius from the violence of the mob, but they seized one unfortunate citizen of the name of Cinna, thinking it a certain Cinna who had been known as an enemy of Caesar. They cut off his head, notwithstanding his shrieks and cries, and carried it about the city on the tip of a pike, a dreadful symbol of their hostility to the enemies of Caesar. As frequently happens, however, in such deeds of sudden violence, these hasty and lawless avengers found afterward that they had made a mistake, and beheaded the wrong man.

Caesar's monument.

The comet.

The Roman people erected a column to the memory of Caesar, on which they placed the inscription, "To THE FATHER OF HIS COUNTRY." They fixed the figure of a star upon the summit of it, and some time afterward, while the people were celebrating some games in honor of his memory, a great comet blazed for seven nights in the sky, which they recognized as the mighty hero's soul reposing in heaven.

Printed in Great Britain
by Amazon